Mission America

Dr. Luauna Stines

L.S. Publishing

Mission America

Mission America
Copyright © 2013 by Dr. Luauna Stines

Scripture quotations are from the New King James Version

ISBN: 978-0-9884172-7-4

Printed in the U.S.A. by
L.S. Publishing
P.O. Box 2800
Ramona, CA 92065

Contact Information:
Or to schedule meetings
Dr. Luauna Stines
drluauna@atouchfromabove.org

Table of Contents

Chapter One .... The Journey Begins 13

Chapter Two .... Life on the Road 21

Chapter Three .... God's Divine Appointments 32

Chapter Four .... Fort Tuthill Military Recreation 39

Chapter Five .... Prescott, Here We Come! 45

Chapter Six .... Location, Location, Location 49

Chapter Seven .... Modern Day Book of Acts 59

Chapter Eight .... Let the Work Begin 67

Chapter Nine .... Lives Touched Forever 85

Chapter Ten .... Trials & Victories 95

Chapter Eleven .... Atlanta: We Made It! 112

Chapter Twelve .... How Can I Explain This? 138

Chapter Thirteen .... Burying the Past 148

Chapter Fourteen .... Tour Two Begins 175

Chapter Fifteen .... God's Majestic Northwest 181

Chapter Sixteen .... Pit Stop in Billings 193

Chapter Seventeen ...... My Birthplace 208

Chapter Eighteen .... When God Takes You Full Circle 219

Chapter Nineteen .... Mission San Diego 246

Dedicated to my Lord & Savior Jesus Christ

Foreword

It is a privilege to recommend Dr. Luauna Stines' ministry and affirm her personal Christian life for ministry. Several healings have followed her preaching that I know of, and possibly many more that I do not know of. Fervency and an anointing of the Holy Spirit are earmarks of her ministry.

It seems apparent that the Holy Spirit has been silently grooming her for a greater ministry because of her strong love for the unsaved. In the meantime, I have been grateful to see results wherever she has preached. Through her ministry, many casual believers have been stirred to seek God for their personal Christian growth and development.

Dr. Stines has an outstanding personal testimony that she shares when the Holy Spirit prompts her to share it. She is a living example of the tremendous grace of God.

I believe the Holy Spirit will leave His mark on the churches where she has ministered. I commend her to you and trust that in God's time your church will have the privilege of her ministry.

Sincerely in Christ,
Lydia Swain (Mrs.)
Former Director of Foreign Affairs and Ministries
for Dr. David Yonggi Cho (13 years)
Yoido Full Gospel Church, Seoul, Korea

Introduction

Ever experience God trying to get your attention? A few years ago, I knew the Holy Spirit was prompting me to step out into the harvest field fulltime. I must admit, I dug my heels in, anchored deep in my job, and then acted as if my ears were deaf to what the Holy Spirit was saying to my heart. Like Jonah, when God told him to go into Nineveh, Jonah went in the opposite direction and headed into Tarshish, I must say God does have a way of getting our attention!

I knew with all my mind the Lord had laid a burden for the United States of America, and our spiritual condition deep within my heart. Since sin is running rampant, America is in need of a Holy Ghost move of God. The Holy Spirit kept speaking to my heart to step out by faith, to go forth throughout the United States and preach His Word. I had already purchased a revival tent years prior to the first time the Lord told me to go into the harvest field!

I made every excuse one could make, everyone of them sounded and even looked like I had a "legit" reason to wait. From owning my own business to the excuse, "I can't Lord, I'm building a place of prayer," and on and on. I was making great money at the business and revenues were increasing as each month passed. Little by little I forgot about the voice of God and His desire; to go forth. I kept right on working hard. Within one year I felt like the rug was pulled right out from underneath me. One day just as fast as I was making money, something happened, a dead stop in my growing finances. As each day passed the income started to dwindle. At first I thought, "This is nothing, it's just a few slow days." Then it continued one month to another, the money was steadily disappearing.

I started getting behind on my house payment, not making enough money to cover the normal month's expenses. I prayed, bound up the devil and stood on the Word of God. Yet, something else was happening and I had no control. As I watched day-to-day, things were getting worse. I thought to myself, "It cannot get any worse!" Well, it did! The San Diego County fires burned through in 2007, once again the fire started in Ramona. The Saturday before was our biggest day of sales, the fire started on Sunday and we were surrounded by flames and engulfed in smoke. Our town was the first to evacuate, all businesses were shut down, the municipal water was shut off, and hundreds of homes went up in flames.

After about a week and a half everyone was trying to get back on track, including myself. As time passed, it was only getting worse, I was making less than $100 a day. I had three workers, a different commercial lot to cover, mortgages, and many other expenses which needed to be met, yet nothing. Ouch! With my entire mind and my heart I was crying out to the Lord.

As I was preparing for my church service, as I did every week, I prayed and studied. The next day, something was different in this service, maybe it went unnoticed by the other people that morning, but I felt the Holy Spirit's presence so strong. Of course, I always welcomed the Holy

Spirit; when I started my teaching all of a sudden I felt as if I was the only one in the room, even though I was surrounded by people. I had just quoted:

> **Luke 5:4-5**, "When He had stopped speaking, He said to Simon, 'Launch out into the deep and let down your nets for a catch.' But Simon answered and said to Him, 'Master, we have toiled all night and caught nothing; nevertheless at Your word I will let down the net.'"

Right after I spoke out those verses, I felt frozen in time and space, the verse was like a hammer to my heart and those words were burning deep within like a branding iron. I wanted to fall right to my knees, and I felt like weeping like a baby. The Holy Spirit's presence surrounded me in a way I had never felt before. I just stood there right in the middle of a Wednesday church service looking towards heaven, and without realizing it I said out loud in front of the congregation, "Yes, Lord. I am so sorry; you are speaking right to my heart." As I stood still looking towards heaven, immobile, tears were falling from my eyes. I realized the state I was in, for no other reason, was caused by my own disobedience. I had ignored what God was so gently speaking to my heart for the several years: _GO FORTH!_

That night at home, I sat on the end of my bed thinking and weeping, I fell to my knees, and wept before the Lord. I did not know how I was going to do it, I just knew I was going to step out to do what the Holy Spirit put in my heart and I was now going to obey His command.

This book is written about a step of faith, __Mission America__. How God used five single women, the least likely, to go out and labor, to touch thousands of people for the Lord's purpose. We covered the southern part of the United States from San Diego, California to Columbia, South Carolina and back on Tour 1. On Tour 2, we covered the western states from San Diego north along the Pacific Ocean, then across to Billings, Montana and circled back home via Wyoming, Colorado, New Mexico, Arizona to home base. I pray your heart will be stirred, and that you will step out by faith, for without faith it is impossible to please Him.

Mission America written from our travel journal as we shared highlights of what, where, when and how our Mighty God moved as we went forth to fulfill His Great Commission. The Lord used wonderful people to bless us all along our path; we were privileged to meet so many new friends on our journey.

Thank you for taking time out, and reading this book, I personally pray you will be encouraged and touched as you see how today our God is able to move on behalf of anyone who is willing to step out and trust Him.

*Jesus Christ is the same yesterday, today and forever."
Hebrews 13:8.*

Now, come along with us on our journey

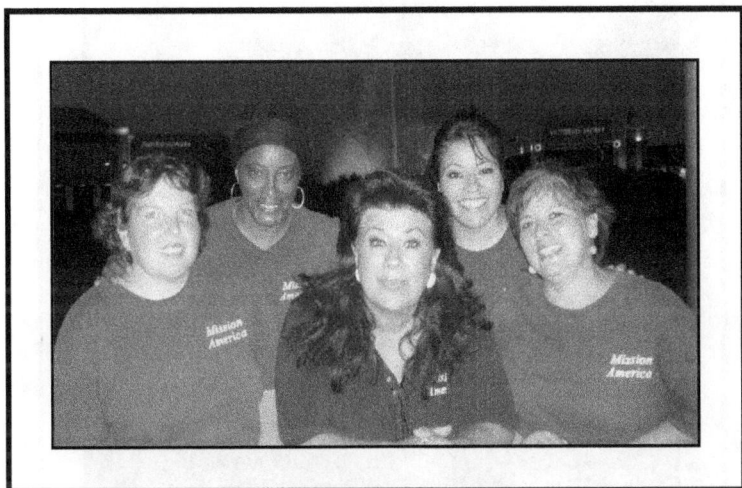

*Mission America Team
Left to right: Jill Campbell, Rhonda Butcher, Dr. Luauna
Stines, Kaweah Stines, Beverly Maes*

The Journey Begins

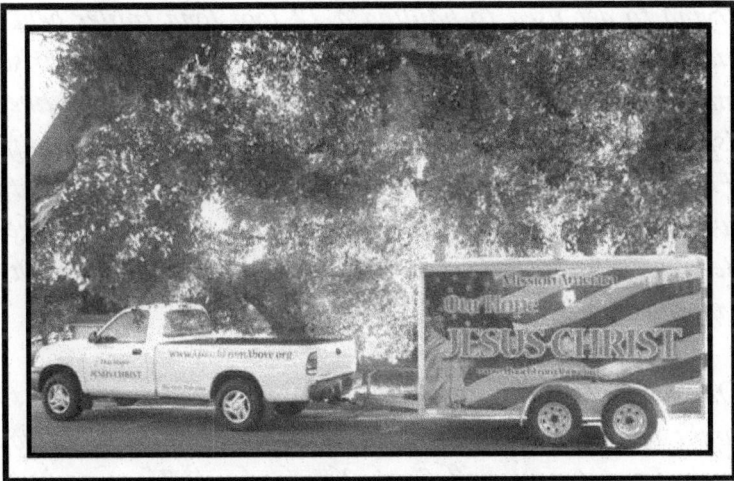

I have traveled around the world including into *Africa* where you automatically pray and trust God for every single thing. This time, our team, five single women are missionaries to our homeland, America our mission field!

We left Ramona, California in San Diego County early on Monday morning, it was Memorial Day. We left by faith with a great task ahead of us, driving away in a Toyota Tundra truck, pulling an enclosed trailer and in Rhonda's Toyota sedan; five single women, four "missionary" puppies and $1,000 cash in our pocket.

San Diego Living Waters Church, gave the $1,000 to start our journey. The night before we left, I prayed to God and said, "If you want us to go, we will need $1,000." The next day the Lord sent Deacon Frank Doan and the church with the money.

I was gripping my steering wheel with white knuckles trying to get used to hauling a 12 foot long trailer behind me. Remember, I have the name, "Our Hope, Jesus Christ," on both sides of the trailer; I was trying not to look like a "spaz" holding tight onto the steering wheel for dear life. Finally, after a hundred or so miles I finally got used to the weight and the feel of pulling a trailer. I was able to take a deep breath and relax; it felt like I just went through a vigorous workout.

Our first plan was to go to Atlanta. I had forgotten the night before, I told the Lord, "I don't want to be in your way, I want your will Lord. You lead us!" Heading in the direction towards Atlanta and after three hours of driving, our second driver in the vehicle behind us, Rhonda, was feeling a little tired. She called on the walkie-talkie and said, "I'm really getting tired, need to switch drivers."

Looking for a sign that would show me how far the next rest stop was, I realized we were in the sand dunes and it was over 110 degrees. Finally, we reached a rest stop just outside of Yuma, Arizona it was Memorial Day. I pulled in cautiously, with my big trailer behind me. As I turned the corner to park, I heard a terrible sound, ever popped a big balloon? I looked through the rear view mirror, thinking I ran over something, what did my eyes behold? One of our brand new tires had blown up and looked as if it had been through WWII. I was not expecting this because I just drove off the trailer lot with this brand new $6,000 trailer thinking I would be "ok," no need to worry about tires.

Jumping out of the vehicle and realizing we were in the middle of the desert, it was HOT! I had remembered we did not have a spare; I was waiting for the next town to buy one. (Mr. George, I should have listened to you before I left, you told me I should buy a spare!) Being the calm leader, trying hard not to panic, both hands went straight in the air, I cried out, "Jesus, I need help!" Five single women, no jack, and no spare. Just as I finished praying, into the rest area drove a beautiful red truck, with a nice trailer, exactly like ours, the only difference was they had a spare! I could see it, the tire was in plain sight.

I frantically waved them down and they pulled over. I said, "Excuse me sir, would you happen to have an extra spare?" Who's going to carry an extra spare? He said, "Nope, just the one we have." I said, "Sir, we're a team of missionaries to America, it's Memorial Day and we're stuck in this HOT desert. I don't know how far the next town is, would you please consider letting us use your spare? You could follow us to the next town to a gas station; I'll give you back your spare tire." His wife panicked, and told her husband, "What about us?" I said, "Ma'am, you can follow us, I don't want to keep your spare, I just know if we don't get to the next town we are going to be stuck in this desert." The husband very quietly said something to her, I moved back because I could tell they were having one of those "husband-wife" conversations. I prayed, "Lord, please put it in their heart, we need a miracle!"

Not wanting to give him too much time to change their mind and leave us, I walked up to the window and asked, "Well, sir, do you know how far the next town is?" He said, "Twenty miles." I said, "Sir, it's a holiday and this is not a coincidence that you drove in right after our tire blew up, your trailer spare tire is the exact tire which fits our trailer." Then he leaned over and whispered to his wife, within seconds he jumped out of his truck. He reached for his jack, pulled his spare off and fixed our tire like an expert. In the meantime, I had Beverly calling around, hunting for a place where we could buy a new tire and have this one fixed. We could not waste any more time.

Thank God for Christian contacts and good friends. Beverly remembered a faithful Christian lady, Ms. Wanda from our town of Ramona who had a son-in-law that lived in Yuma. Ms. Wanda called him immediately and he gave us the list of all locations which were open and could fix the tire in his city. By this time the guy had finished putting his spare on our trailer and he asked, "Where are we headed?" We told him the name of the store and he said, "Here give me the address, I have a GPS, follow me and I'll lead you right in."

Within minutes, we were back on the road, following another truck and a trailer. We were "chauffeured" into Yuma by this couple, who were active duty Army, both working in the Intelligence Field at Fort Huachuca. I could tell they were trained soldiers because they wasted no time, they were people of action!

After we pulled into the tire store to get our tire fixed, we now had time to witness, and share God's love with this wonderful couple who came to rescue us, on angel's wings. We discovered, the beautiful woman soldier was raised with an incredible mother and father, who were missionaries to South America. She was backslidden, and her husband just began his search for God. Our meeting was God ordained! I shared how much God loved her. You could see she was almost in tears, the young lady's parents must have been praying for years for the return of their daughter to the Lord. Her husband was so open; I was able to explain to him how to become a Christian.

I realized we needed to buy a spare tire before we started driving again. Right next door to the Pep Boys Tire store was Lowes, we purchased a spare, drove out of the parking lot with our new tire. We lost four hours out of our day, or did we really lose them? The Holy Spirit had a plan for this couple, the husband's name was written in the Lamb's Book of Life.

We headed on the road again to find a campground for the night, we were going through the winding roads from Yuma towards Phoenix. Once again I found myself gripping the steering wheel. "Maybe after a week or so, I won't be gripping the steering wheel so tightly," I thought to myself. Time was passing fast and it was getting late, I knew our campground was in an area that would be hard to find in the dark, so we went directly there.

We found the campsite, squeezed into our little parking area, and found our cabin keys. The darkness was settling in over us while we unloaded and prepared everything for the night. Rhonda claimed the top bunk, Jill claimed the bottom, Kaweah and I claimed the queen bed, Beverly stood there with her gear in hand saying, "Guess what, I claim the floor!" Seeing how there were no other beds; five single women in one little 12' x 12' KOA Campground Cabin, imagine it. Did I forget to tell you our four little "missionary" dogs were with us too? They claimed everyone's bed!

Finally, getting a chance to catch our breath after setting up our beds, we went outside looked at the campfire and said, "Alright, let's have dinner. Who packed the food?" We all looked at each other and discovered we were fasting for the night, we forgot to pack food! I remembered I had a little container of raw carrots, so we had a carrot with some drinking water and thanked God for the wonderful gentleman and his wife, Tom and Julie, who came to rescue us that day with their spare tire.

How could I forget to share with you, during our first day adventure, a precious Indian woman named, Maxine gave her heart to the Lord. Boris also was saved, he was a clerk at the first gas station before we crossed the California border into Arizona. Daniel and his beautiful wife and sister-in-law gave their hearts to the Lord at the rest area where our tire blew out right outside of Yuma. Gusto a customer at the Pep Boys tire store also was saved. Mr. Dwayne and Jeri outside of McDonald's near the last gas station of the day between Phoenix and Black Canyon City. Our first day report also includes all the other witnessing we did during the day; at every stop people would ask us, "What are you doing? What is Mission America?" Jesus was boldly shared, and His name was lifted up all day. At the end of night, it was late I was too tired to write anymore in my journal. Thank you Jesus, you are so GOOD to us!

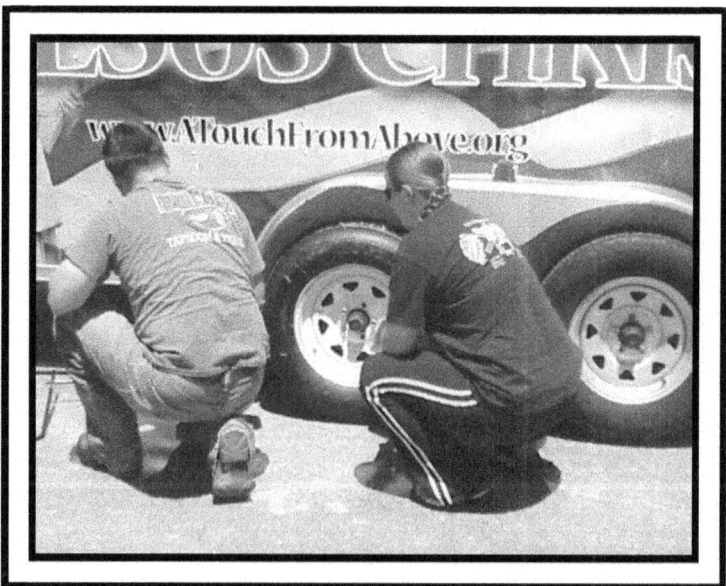

Chapter Two
Mission America Journey

Life on the Road

I woke up early and my body was screaming, "Ouch!" The mattress was as comfortable as sleeping on a rock thus I was as stiff as a board. I rose out of bed with the mission in mind so we started packing our gear. Jill always faithful to make coffee went hunting for some wood, she started a fire, pulled out the old campfire coffee pot and before you knew it, you could hear it perking. We all continued to pack as the coffee was brewing. When it was finished, Jill served coffee to everyone; she smiled and said, "Oops, we forgot the sugar and the cream." The same way we forgot the food the day before, we all just laughed; we prayed and thanked God for the day.

Just then a lady walked up to the porch at the front of our cabin. The lady was kind of fancy. Beverly found out she was born in Israel. She was on a camping vacation with her husband, they had rented a motor home and were driving around Arizona. Her husband was English and they were visiting America from their home in England. In her hands, she had a few cans of soup and some tuna. She said, "We're flying out this afternoon," and asked, "Would you ladies like to have this food?" We all smiled and knew it was an open door to share Jesus. She smiled as we told her how the Lord used her to supply our breakfast. She said, "Do you want to know the real miracle? I offered the food to a few other trailers before I asked you, obviously the others refused."

Isn't God amazing? He sent a couple all the way from England on vacation to meet us at a campground which we were not planning to stay at, to provide us with food. The rest of the story is, this beautiful lady was wide open to the gospel and she prayed a sincere prayer to receive Jesus Christ before we parted ways. We opened up a can of soup and had soup with the coffee, what a breakfast!

As we were finishing up the last bit of coffee, the team started packing the trailer and vehicles. Everyone was scurrying to clean up the campsite when Jill said, "Pastor, you need to come and look at this." As she took me to the side of the trailer and said, "Look." Sure enough, it was another tire going flat, "Oh no, not another tire!" Jill pulled out the air pump and started to pump it up. I told everyone "Hurry, load everything up, fast!" We had to find a place to fix the second tire and quickly because it was losing air fast. Remember, we were nowhere close to a major city or town.

As we left the KOA Campground I realized I could only drive 15 miles an hour. Someone at the campground said there might be a little service station just across the freeway overpass. We headed in that direction only to discover a little hole in the wall gas station and attached convenience store. It looked straight out of the "Twilight Zone," complete with a man dressed in a dirty western, full length coat sitting on a bench outside. As soon as we drove in and he saw the words, "Jesus Christ," he started talking to himself, using foul language and yelling, I thought he might even start foaming at the mouth, this is no exaggeration.

Jill pulled out the air pump which plugged into the cigarette lighter and filled the tire up again. I asked the lady, "Ma'am, we have to find help, is there anything close by so we don't' have to drive down the freeway?" She answered, "There may be something about a mile down the frontage road."

Off we went, driving slowly down the frontage road, looking and praying, "Lord, we need another miracle!" A mile down the road we found a service station operated by a young man named Shane. He looked at us, noticed our great big trailer he had a strange little smirk on his face and I noticed a different look in his eye. I walked in and said, "Hello, I need some help, can you help me with my tire?" He answered, "Give me a little time, I'm working on this customer right now, it will be about 10 minutes." Now remember, this is the second tire to go flat, in two days.

The other gentleman who was getting his tire fixed looked like a genuine, good old cowboy. He was a horse trainer and horse breaker; he stood and looked at me right in the eye,

23

this country adventure took place in Black Canyon City, Arizona.

All three of us just kind of looked at each other; the silence was deafening. I started up a conversation; I wanted to find the opportunity to witness. I said, "So sir, how long have you been training horses?" He answered, "Ever since I was a little one." I then asked, "Do they call you the Horse Whisperer?" He looked outside and saw the trailer, turned back in and took a spit of the tobacco he was chewing, never answering the question. I said, "Pretty nice trailer, huh?" He just looked at me, nodded his head and spit again. I said, "My name is Dr. Luauna, we are A Touch From Above Ministries, a Christian Missionary Team, going across the entire United States on a mission to share Jesus. How about you cowboy, do you go to church?" I think he was a little shocked, he replied, I believe in God," and he spit again. I smiled and posed the question, "Sir, the devil believes in God too and shudders, but do you know Jesus as your Savior?" He responded, "Well, I kind of know him," and spit again only this time I moved out of the way. I continued, "Sir, kinda knowing Him and knowing Him are two different things, the Bible says, "You must be born again."

I noticed Shane glancing at me now and then through the entire conversation, I asked him, "How about you Shane?" I figured I might as well drag him into our conversation as well. He looked at me with those piercing blue eyes, I could tell, he had been hurt, broken and he was just a little bit angry inside. He just kind of smirked and said nothing. I continued on with my conversation with the cowboy and told him, "Well, cowboy, Jesus wants to be your Lord, can I pray with you right now?" He was getting as nervous as a "cat on a hot tin roof". He didn't want to deny Christ and he didn't want to accept Christ. It's hard being a wild bronco rider and walking on a tightrope! I said to the cowboy, "Sir, you gotta make a decision, that's probably why I'm here today." He kind of smiled and said, "Maybe I'll just go to the other place where all my friends are, so we can hang out and party." I told him, "There is no party in hell, its total darkness with the wailing and gnashing of teeth. The Lord will bring to your remembrance, this day May 26th. The day when a wild, woman preacher pulling a trailer with "Our Hope Jesus Christ" on it crossed your path and you refused." Just about the time I finished the last sentence, old Shane jumped in and joined our conversation.

As Shane was finishing up the cowboy's truck, he said, "That ain't the God I know, I don't believe that God would send anybody to hell. I don't believe there is a hell" I said, "You're right Shane, God doesn't want to send anyone to hell, that's why He sent Jesus to die on the cross; but we have to receive Him as Savior." Then I explained to him about the plan of salvation, being born-again. Shane said, "I don't believe in all that stuff, I don't believe that Jesus is the only way." The Holy Spirit instantly spoke to my heart, revealing to me that Shane had a Jehovah Witness background. I asked, "So, Shane, are you a Jehovah Witness? It sounds to me like you still have a lot of that doctrine in you." He answered, "I used to be, but I found God in my own way." I said, "Shane, Jesus loves you!" Then I began to share my testimony; how my husband was murdered and how I was a single mother raising two children, my story softened his heart. He said with hurt in his voice, "I'm a single dad, raising my little boy who is 12 years old." I told him, "I have great respect for you being such a good dad."

I could feel the Holy Spirit continuing to soften his heart, God sent me there for Shane. He later told me, "I used to be a Christian, but all that religion turned me off." I said, "Shane, religion turned Jesus off, He loves you and cares a lot about you. I want to leave you my book so you can read more of my story; I am a miracle of God's grace." By this time the cowboy had already gone and it was just Shane and I. The Holy Spirit was doing a deep work in him. He finished my tire and I asked him, "What do I owe you?" He looked at me with those screaming blue eyes and waved his hand, motioning me to get out of there, he covered the expenses. I shook his hand and thanked him, told him there was a really good church in Flagstaff. A church which was not caught up with a bunch of religion and laws, I gave him the address and we said our goodbyes.

Now I was driving down the road with confidence, "Whew, yeah, the tire was fixed!" No more than 35 minutes later, we were on a major pass in the middle of nowhere, when tire number three started to lose air. We pulled over on the freeway; I looked at the tire and began talking to God again, "Lord, I know we must be on the right track, tire number three?" Jill pulled out the faithful little tire pump and filled up the tire. We jumped in the truck fast because we needed to get to the next town. We were on a steep hill, so we could not change the tire ourselves. I could only drive fast enough to crawl up the mountain and I prayed all the way, "Lord, keep the air in the tire, Lord, keep the air in the tire!"

There was no town in sight, but thank God for Dr. Laurie's gift before we left, he gave us a GPS, Beverly, went to work again. Beverly was in the second car which was following the trailer, she found a tire shop, the only dilemma was, it was located in a city called Camp Verde, the next small town on the highway to Flagstaff. I said, "Let's go now!"

We made it! We pulled into the tire shop with tire problem number three. The worker from Tire Pro named Craig said, "Ma'am, come take a look," as he pointed at the fourth tire, "this tire is going to be flat as well." He was talking about tire number four too. I was perplexed and asked, "Why are these tires dying on me?" He looked at the dates and said, "Ma'am these are old tires." I asked, "How old?" He said, "2004 and 2005," and he showed me the dates. I said, "Oh-oh, that's not good." I got on the phone and called the trailer company in San Diego County where we bought the trailer. The call was overdue, after all it was our fourth tire in just two days, and I had just bought the trailer days before we left Ramona. The owner of Tire Pro and his crew did everything they could to help. They called the trailer manufacturer, who then called me directly. We worked out a plan and they purchased four brand new tires for me. Praise the Lord!

As our tires were being fixed, I was able to share with the owner of Tire Pro, Don Hanks about our mission. In spite of our bad tires, how the Lord was working miracle after miracle. He was fairly excited about our purpose as I took

27

him to our website. He smiled and asked, "You girls had lunch yet?" He didn't know we only had a half a cup of soup and a cup of coffee before our multi-tire episode. I looked at the clock and realized it was 1:30 p.m., can you imagine all morning and three tires out? I responded, "No, but we'll get lunch after all the tires are on." He looked at me and said, "I want to buy you all lunch. Go across the street, there's a little restaurant there, lunch is on me." I smiled, as I thought "Truly, God has a plan." I said, "Thank you sir, that is very kind of you." They finished up our tires and we went across the street. I guess I have to admit we were all hungry, carrots and water the night before, a half a cup of soup and coffee in morning. At this rate, we just might get skinny on this trip.

Sitting down at the restaurant there was a gentleman, Ken and his wife, Trisha who kept looking at us, they noticed the Mission America t-shirts we were wearing. After a few glances, I felt compelled to introduce myself. I found out he was a Christian, a cyclist and very excited about our mission; they came and joined us at our table. What a wonderful couple, we shared about the goodness of God and all the Lord had done in such a short time. Ken shared how he wanted to bicycle across the U.S. and tell everyone about Jesus. I laughed with joy and said, "Life is short, just do it!"

Towards the end of the meal, I found out they lived in Prescott, as the name of their city came out of their mouth, the Holy Spirit leapt in my heart, He was leading me. Our first destination was settled, Prescott, Arizona, I decided we would hold our first tent meeting there. Meeting Ken and Trisha was another confirmation. The first indication was from Dr. Bruce Laurie; before we left San Diego, Dr. Laurie, said, "I own a lot in Prescott, Arizona, you can use it for your tent meetings if you like." Amazing how God works! The couple said, "We're going to come to your tent meeting, do you need help?" Of course, we welcome all help and looked forward to seeing them again when we arrive in Prescott.

We said our goodbyes, gave each other hugs then Ken reached out for his wallet and said, "I want to invest in your mission." Ken placed $40 in my hand; he didn't know he was paying for our next overnight stay at the KOA Campground. Blessings to Ken and Trisha, I said a prayer for God to bless them. We would see them soon in their city, when we set up for our tent meeting.

Once I made the decision for our Prescott Tent Meeting, we started planning. We called Dr. Laurie for the exact address of his lot and Beverly went to work to find a men's Christian home in the city to help us set up the tent upon our arrival. Praise God, within minutes we found, Church on the Street Men's home, a kind man named Wes did not hesitate at our request, he said, "Give me a call when you need the men and tell me how many you need." Praise the Lord!

Orders finalized from the Holy Spirit, we were off to the KOA Campground in Flagstaff. Our report from that day alone on May 26th those who received Christ as Savior: Ariella, the Jewish woman who gave us canned foods at the

Black Canyon City KOA. Mr. Floyd an elderly man eating at Crusty's Pizza in Camp Verde.

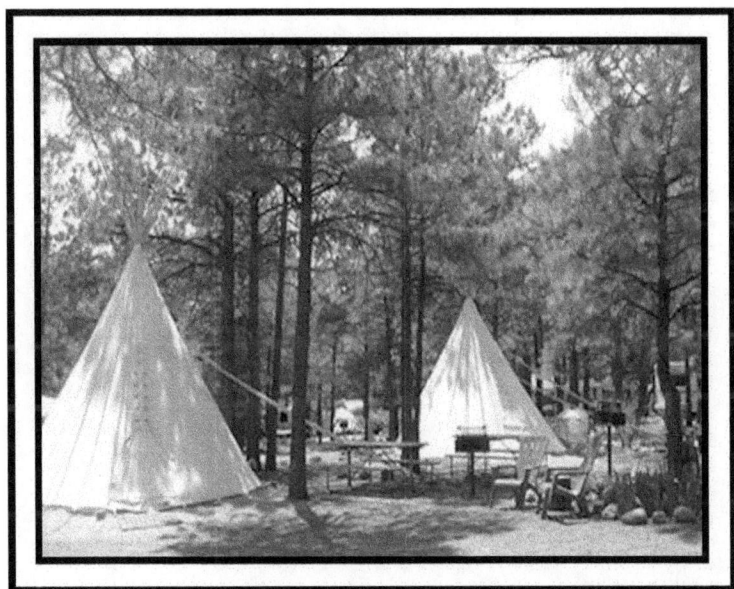

Chapter Three
Mission America Journey

God's Divine Appointments

*W*e arrived in Flagstaff late Tuesday afternoon May 26th, our stop before heading to Prescott. We had time to prepare our bunks, unpack, and get a nice, hot shower. I planned to visit a friend's church, Pastor Weidinger of Grace Fellowship Christian Center on Wednesday night. I could not come this close and not stop in, we would surprise them and visit their service to say, "Hello." We had a full day to regroup and accomplish what needed to be done, it was nice after the stress of the first two days, I needed a little rest from all the tire problems.

The door opened for our tent meeting to be done in Prescott, Arizona first, and then we planned to head to Atlanta, Georgia, Lord willing of course. I was excited to watch God unfold the every detail and plan for the Prescott Tent Meeting.

I woke up early on Wednesday, May 27th and we decided

to go out and find a place to sit down, have coffee and eat breakfast. The waitress at Coco's was being trained and saw our shirts; she said, "I used to go to youth group when I was younger." I shared with her how much Jesus loved her. She was so touched and when we were leaving she came up to me and asked me to please pray for her friend, who was going through rehab. I told her we would pray, and she said she would go to church. I gave her Grace Fellowship Christian Center's address and Pastor Weidinger's name, she said, "I will go to church on Sunday."

Back at our campground I found some precious time to write. I sat down, finally having time for my mind to rest. I felt the Holy Spirit's presence so strong it brought me to tears. I looked around because I could not stop crying. I was absolutely amazed, "Wow, finally," I thought to myself. We worked so hard for such a long time to prepare for Mission America, it had been a dream in my heart for many years. An overwhelming gratefulness came upon me, like a warm, cozy blanket of God's love. I was especially thankful for how Jesus surrounded me with wonderful people. I could not stop the tears, "Thank you Jesus!" All I could do was cry; it didn't matter about the four blown tires. Meeting these wonderful people, who were heaven sent, minimized the trials.

We decided to head towards Prescott, Arizona on Thursday, May 28th. Everywhere we went people were amazed at the message of our "Jesus" trailer and our mission. This day is just the beginning of great things, God always shows Himself faithful.

The report of those who prayed to receive Christ on May 27th were: two seven year old boys at the playground; Scott and Bradon. We stayed at the same KOA two more nights.

We mingled around the Flagstaff KOA Campground sharing Jesus with everyone for the few days we stayed there. It was a beautiful KOA in the middle of pine trees, the landscaping was immaculate, the scenery reminded me of Colorado, actually Flagstaff is a sister city to Colorado Springs where I grew up. At the same time, we were trying to catch up on business papers which took me most of the morning on our departure date, Thursday, May 28th.

I sat at a picnic table with an umbrella in one hand, because of the sporadic rainfall and I had to use the computer outside, the maid service needed to clean the cabin for the next guest. The team was busy packing, cleaning, and preparing to leave the campground because our cabin was rented for the night.

The lady across from our little cabin, smiled as she saw us with all of our t-shirts, she walked over and said, "I am a Christian." She asked me, "What are you doing?" I shared with her about our mission and she started to tear up. She said, "I am so touched because America is in great need. I sit on my Mission Board at church and I'm going to tell them about your mission and ask them to get behind you. While we support missions all around the world, America goes to hell." She waved her hand to try to stop the tears, she was so moved. I told her about our trailer and she said, "I'm going to go get my camera and take a picture of it." Sure enough, she did, she came back a few hours later, when we were closing up and said, "Again, I'm so touched by your mission." She reached out and gave me $40 and said, "This is all I have on me right now, I want to bless your mission." She didn't know she was paying for our next campground. I gave her one of my books, and Kaweah sang her a song. I told the girls to get one of Kaweah's CD's, "*He Is Risen*," and I gave it to her, her name was Jackie, what a blessing to meet her.

While we were getting ready to leave the campground, a friend named Azalea called, Beverly was rejoicing when she heard. Azalea had invited us over for Mexican food, Beverly smiled from ear-to-ear and said, "Hallelujah, a hot dinner, that's God!" Azalea offered us rooms in her house to stay the night. Once again Beverly jumped for joy; after all she has slept on the floor for three nights. I asked Beverly, "Did you tell her we had four missionary dogs?" Her answer was, "I forgot." I said, "Call her back; she needs to know about the puppies." Beverly came back walking really slow with her head hanging low, "I guess it's not God, she has two Akita-Chow dogs who take pleasure in killing other small animals; including all cats and small dogs." No wonder they had two acres, and their property was double fenced, so much for homemade Mexican food, and comfortable beds.

When we drove out of the KOA campground, we were amazed, people were yelling from all directions, from other cabins and tent sites "God bless you," "See you later," "Blessings on you, grace of God be with you!" I felt like we were in a parade, it made me smile and I felt great joy in my heart.

35

Our friend Azalea did meet us in the parking lot of OfficeMax to say hello and look at the trailer. Right after Azalea arrived, we saw a young man crossing the street directly in front of us. He had earphones in his ear and a black t-shirt with blood dripping off the words, which read, "Cannibal Corpse," it must have been a band. Beverly ran to catch him. She told him when Jesus was here, he did not go around saying, "Jesus, loves you,' he said, 'Repent for the kingdom of God is at hand!'" She could smell the alcohol on his breath and it was only lunch time. She asked him if he knew what repent meant. He gave the correct biblical explanation, so she knew he was brought up in church. He prayed and repented and came to say, "Hello," to the whole group. It was God's perfect timing, once again. Our friend Azalea, who lives in Flagstaff was still there. We gave her his name, number and address so she could follow up on him. He was grateful.

We did not know our next campground location and the raindrops continued and their intensity increased as we saw dark clouds coming over the horizon. We had to stop at Wal-Mart to pick up an extra tent and a few things we needed. As we were standing in the line to check out, directly behind us was a beautiful young woman, probably no more than 28 years old. She placed her items on the check stand, she was buying three packs of shot glasses. Jill and I looked at her, looked at the shot glasses, then at each other. Jill pulled out one of our little gospel tracts which said, "Jesus is coming back. Are you ready?"

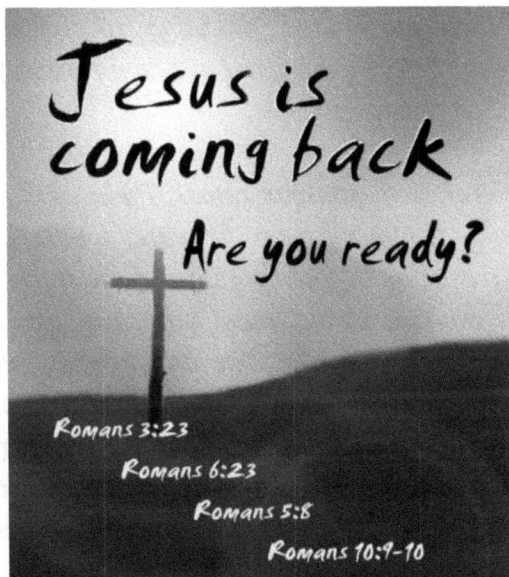

Jesus is coming back

Are you ready?

Romans 3:23
Romans 6:23
Romans 5:8
Romans 10:9-10

Jill told her, "You know, I used to drink everyday." The young lady became obviously a little nervous and started smiling. She looked at the shot glasses, looked at Jill and sheepishly said, "These aren't for me!" Jill just smiled and said, "Yeah, that's what I used to say." Jill's testimony warmed the young woman's heart.

We walked out of the Wal-Mart store together and we were able to complete the witness. When we got outside the door, the girl was tearing up as she said, "This is weird, I went to two churches searching for God, but I was afraid. After I tried those two churches I said, 'Just forget it, I'll read my Bible and do this on my own.'" We led her to Jesus right there walking out the door at Wal-Mart in Flagstaff, this was definitely God's appointment with her! Once again, we referred her Pastor Wiedinger's church, we wrote down the church name, address and service times and asked her to go there on Sunday. Amazing, to everything under God's heaven there is a time and a season for everything and everyone, Ecclesiastes 3:1.

Have you ever seen monsoon rains? These were not normal rains; it's like God opened up the water fountain of heaven and it poured straight down. We heard the storm was going to last for hours and we found out there was a military recreational facility in the same direction as our route to Prescott. By this time, most of the day was gone. I could not see driving a few hours not knowing our next location in this crazy rain. I told Beverly to get the directions to the military recreation facility and that's where we headed.

What an exciting stay in Flagstaff! While we were at the KOA we had the privilege of praying with two 14 year old girls we had met in the bathroom. Cynthia who needed prayer for her beautiful 5 year old daughter whom she adopted, the little girl was oppressed by rejection and the curse of generations. Krista prayed to receive Jesus at Wal-Mart. Dallas prayed in the parking lot of OfficeMax. Eight year old Destiny prayed in the bathroom before we left the campground. Praise the Lord for every one of those souls! God is good. I'm still gripping the steering wheel.

Fort Tuthill Military Recreation

*W*hen we arrived, we found out the cabins were too expensive so we planned to rent tent sites and sleep in our tents. As we were driving to our campsite, I looked around the corner and saw a small yurt, the same kind we are planning to build on the Prayer Mountain. I went back to the front desk and asked for the cost. We found out we could rent a yurt for $25, only problem, no dogs allowed in the yurt. We started unpacking, set up our bedding and figured out we would put our dog cage on the deck of the yurt.

Great idea, until the man from the front desk saw our dog cage on the deck. He was the same person who already had a problem with us the minute he saw our t-shirts. Actually he had a problem with the name of Jesus, period. He was sarcastic and rude the moment we walked into the office.

Later that day, he came flying over, his large body stuffed in a mini two-seater golf cart, four wheeling up the little road to where our yurt was. He dropped his voice into low gear and scared Kaweah, "Get those dogs off the porch; you are going to have to leave!" I knew our dogs were not the issue, we were surrounded by a Great Dane, two Chows, an English Springer Spaniel and a bunch of Chihuahuas. There is just something about the powerful name of Jesus which should bring out the best in people. Unfortunately, it does bring out the worst too, they either love ya or hate ya!

He left in his little cart down the windy little road, golf cart tilting to one side, back to the office. I returned to the computer room where Beverly was waiting for me and we finished up some work. She went to fax the documents when he noticed her t-shirt, and once again, he put his voice into low gear, "Are you with that group in the yurt? No dogs on the porch, do you understand?" I heard him from the other room, and I knew he was picking on us. I sat and prayed for about 60 seconds, waited for Beverly to come back, I told her, "Finish up the work I'll be right back."

I walked out the door to the desk as calmly as I could. I looked him right in the eye and asked, "Can I have the name of your manager and phone number, Sir?" He looked at me and said, "Why?" I said because I need it right now, may I get the name and number of your manager, Sir." He looked at me and I could tell he was getting a little nervous, I said, "We are a team of five single women and I'm not going to throw one of the young ladies in a tent in a far corner of your campground, in this rain. I'm going to put those dogs on the ground in a cage and I'm going to set a tent right

40

next to my yurt. Can I please have the number to your manager, Sir?" I could tell we were in for a stare down, I felt like I was in a Clint Eastwood movie, the good, the bad, and the ugly...doo...doo...dooo! He backed down and said, "Ok, that's fine." I said, "Thank you; I won't need the manager's name and number after all."

By this time, Kaweah was all shook up, "What are we gonna do? They are going to kick us out, it's raining!" Kaweah was in a panic, she was dragging the tent down the road to the far away tent site in the rain. I got Jill and Kaweah, "Come on back here, it's all settled." We repositioned the tent and put the dog cage inside the tent. Beverly headed inside the tent with her bed gear and extra blankets; she was going to sleep in the doggie motel tent. By the way, the rain continued on throughout most of the day.

We woke up the next morning at 4:45 am to freezing temperatures. I heard a noise outside, only to find Beverly walking the dogs. They were shaking like little leaves in the wind. I exclaimed, "My goodness, its cold!" She said, "It was so cold the dogs were freezing. I woke up at 1 am, gave the dogs my blankets, bundled them up in their cage, then I headed to the office." When I looked at Beverly, I realized she had on her white flowered pajamas, purple hat and a white sweater. Thank God no one was at the office, only the graveyard desk clerk. I don't know who had it better, Beverly in the warm office or us in the freezing yurt, thank God we were all out of the rain!

I knew we had to get to Prescott to prepare for our first tent meeting, even though it was Friday morning. It was

41

important for us to find a campground, so we could get organized. While I was at the main office; uploading our journal report for the team back home at the Prayer Mountain and faxing some final paperwork, I noticed they served free coffee. I thought to myself, "Yee haw!" It didn't take long to get my cup, I went out of the coffee area back to do some writing, then went back in to get my second cup of coffee. I was just wondering to God, "Well, Lord, what are we going to have for breakfast?" It rained all night so we did not have any dry wood to make a campfire. As I reached for the coffee pot, right beside the coffee maker was a beautiful platter, there were exactly five beautiful, fresh, unbelievable bagels, two bananas a little thing of cream cheese, and in beautiful writing, the word, "Free." I just smiled, I know the food plate was not there just five minutes earlier. I said, "Beverly come here, call the girls, God has provided our breakfast." Isn't God good? Matthew 6:11, says, "Give us this day our daily bread." Jesus did just that, God shows Himself always faithful!

While checking out, there was a pretty, wild young girl working at the desk. On her forearm from the wrist to the elbow, there was tattooed a wild horse. I mentioned to her, "Pretty nice horse." She smiled, laughed and said, "Not wicked enough." She said, "This horse looks like a Barbie Doll horse, it was supposed to look like the headless horseman's' horse, WICKED." I knew right then, I needed to witness to her. I said, "Wicked? Girl, why do you want wicked?" I told her right away, "Jesus loves you, you wild girl! I used to be a wild girl, but Jesus changed my whole life, God can use you. Have you ever received Jesus?" She answered, "No, but when I was little they dunked me in

42

water." I asked, "Do you mean you were baptized?" She answered, "Yeah, if that's what you call it." I laughed, and said, "Here let me lead you to Jesus."

She looked at me, had a tear in her eye and a nervous little laugh, "My grandmother would love you," she said. I told her, "A grandmother who prays shakes heaven, and changes a nation. That's why I'm here today, your grandmother's been praying for you." Her cool front was rapidly melting away; I reached my hand over the counter and said, "It's time to get saved." She knew exactly what I was saying. I gave her the address of Pastor Weidinger's church and said; "This is the church to go to, ok," then I said goodbye.

Everybody loaded into the car and truck, I walked around the trailer to make sure everything was in order; locks on the doors, the hitch secured, the back of the truck tied down correctly. Everything was "a-o-k" and thank God the skies were clear. We headed on the road towards Prescott, on Interstate 40. What a beautiful drive. When we stopped to fill up with gas, I noticed a few snow capped mountains, no wonder we were freezing. As we drove closer to Prescott, the scenery was even more beautiful; unbelievable cumulus, silver, white lined gray-to-dark-gray clouds. It was like God had a whole bunch of cotton balls up there. You don't see much of those in San Diego. There were deer on the right side of the freeway, pine trees and cedars everywhere; I wish you could have been there to see; the landscape itself is more proof of how awesome our God and His Creation is!

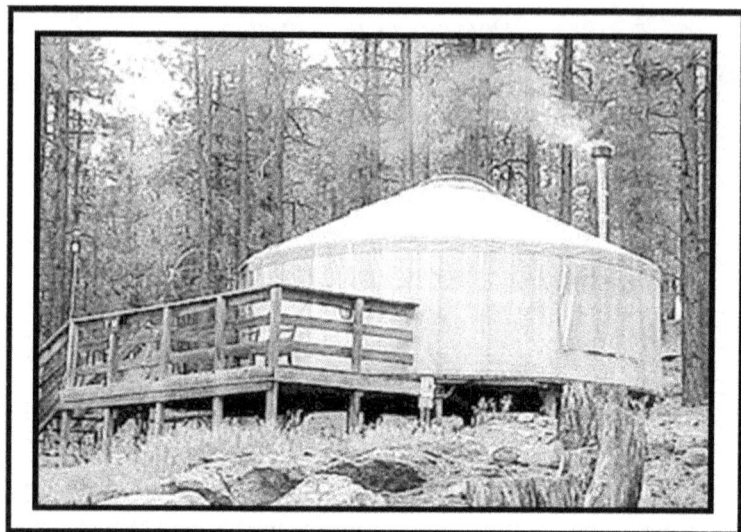

Chapter Five
Mission America Journey

Prescott, Here We Come!

*W*e arrived in Prescott about 11:30 am on Friday, May 29th. We parked the truck and I started calling around for a campground, almost every single one of them was booked, and guess what, no cabins available for a decent price. Hotels were running between $70 to over $150 a night, we needed to find a place for a week to prepare for our tent meeting and I was not going to pay those prices. As I looked up in the sky I could tell those clouds were coming in again, I prayed to myself, "Praise the Lord, in everything give Him praise." I left Kaweah, Rhonda and the four dogs with the truck because time was of the essence. I jumped in Rhonda's car, found a map of Prescott and a phone book and started the search. Up and down and around we went, what a beautiful little town.

We were running out of time, I realized this is why we bought a tent the day before, there was only one campground; they at least had showers and electricity. Ok, so it was a little scary; there were a few people who reminded me of characters right out of the Bible. It was like meeting Legion or Mary Magdalene, troubled souls, with minds confused and in bondage to unseen forces of darkness.

At the same time, we found a bright spot in the middle of this place. One of the workers at the Willow RV Park looked like Grizzly Adams; he was sitting in a golf cart dressed for Arizona weather; a hat to protect him from the sun, shorts, and a t-shirt. Something was different about him; he had a sparkle in his blue eyes. When he saw our t-shirts, he asked, "What is Mission America?" We told him with confidence who we were, we did not want to be confused with Mormon missionaries, who are known for their mission work. I asked him, "What about you? Are you a Christian?" He answered, "Yes," without wavering and welcomed us to Prescott.

After we checked in, he came by our first tent site to see if we were all right, when he stood up he towered over me at 6'4". He asked if I wanted to see his photo album, he said he was a photographer. His photos were incredible! The landscapes were beautiful, it takes an artist's eye for the quality of Larry's gorgeous pictures. You never know who you are going to meet at a campground. I've realized on our journey, the Lord has treasures hidden everywhere.

They put us in the farthest end of the campground saying this is the best place for tents; I have to admit it was a beautiful location. Then I heard a familiar humming sound, which I recognized from my many years of camping. I said,

"Ladies, you better pull out the Skin-So-Soft and OFF, the humming sound was a swarm of mosquitoes, they're coming in for a smorgasbord and we were on the menu." Just about the time I finished the sentence, I got bit behind the ear, on my cheek, my ankle, my forearm and on my hand. Kaweah was making a mad dash for the Skin-So-Soft, I thought she was bringing it to me; instead she instantly rubbed all the dogs down. I said, "Help, I'm being attacked somebody come and rescue me!" Beverly was taking a bath in the Skin-So-Soft, and rubbing herself down as fast as she could. Then she politely asked me, "Pastor, did you need this?" She said, "Oh my, you got bit up!" One hand was frantically swatting the mosquitoes, the other hand trying to rub on the Skin-So-Soft. I think the mosquitoes thought I was dessert.

Rhonda was squirming up and down, side to side, I asked, "Rhonda, are you ok?" She yelled, "Yes!" Then in an instant, she ran like lightning. I called out after her, "Where are you going?" She said, "I gotta go!" She ran behind a bush and made her own squat pot. Funny, when she came out from behind the bush, she was smiling from ear-to-ear. I said, "I hope you put Skin-So-Soft on that bottom." She explained, "I had to go."

We were there for about two hours, set up all our tents and everyone had to go to the bathroom. We realized they might as well have set us up in China, there was no phone reception, we were surrounded by poison oak and the bathrooms were way to far away from us. We headed back to the office. Kaweah felt very uneasy about our location, she said, "Mom, I'm a little nervous, it looks like a scary area." I didn't want to tell her I passed a half-a-dozen

47

really strange people who made faces, talked to themselves and became agitated when they saw "Jesus Christ," on our shirts.

We headed to the office and I looked around. I pleaded with the camp manager, "Sir, please give us a closer campsite; closer to the bathrooms and civilization." He was a little bit hesitant, I said a quick prayer under my breath, "Lord, give us favor." Finally, he nodded and said, "Ok."

By this time, Beverly had already conked out in the little tent, snoring like a freight train from not sleeping the night before. Jill had already gathered wood and was preparing for fire when I walked up and said, "We're moving girls." We decided, we didn't want to tear down the tents all the way, so each of us picked up a corner of one of the domed tents, and marched about a half a mile carrying it all the way to the new location. What a sight.

Our final tent site destination was now just a hop, skip and a jump away from the bathrooms and water. We also realized there were not as many mosquitoes. The camp manager didn't tell us, at our first location, just right over the hill was a lake, what do you think mosquitoes like? Water!

Only Amber prayed to receive Jesus on May 29th in Prescott, even though we did witness to about 30 people total between all our stops on the way to Prescott. We were doing our job and we pray the Holy Spirit will draw them to the cross. This was a glorious day, Amen!

Chapter Six
Mission America Journey

Location, Location, Location

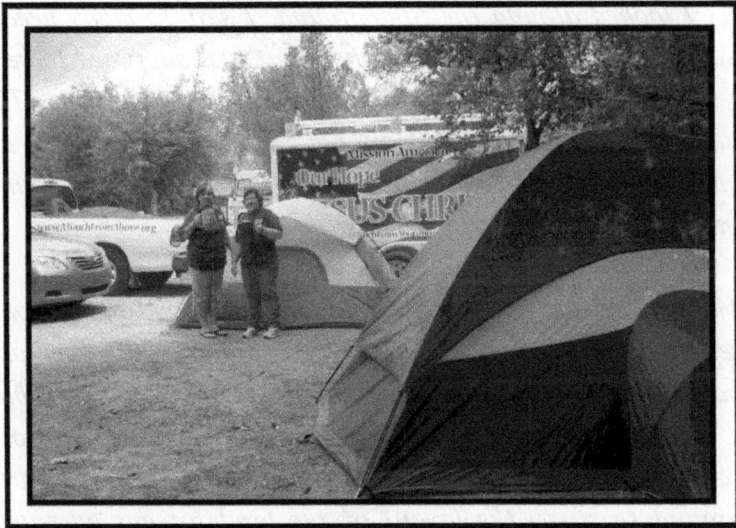

I was up at 4:45 am again on Saturday, May 30th and was very excited to set up our first tent meeting in Arizona. Upon our arrival the previous day, I saw a parking lot in front of an Assembly of God church as we

49

drove into Prescott. I thought the location might be perfect, it's always nice to work with a Spirit-filled church then the new Christians will have a place to grow in the Lord. We went back to the church to find someone. I found a young man named Adam; he was the Youth Pastor and he had a wonderful Spirit. We shared with him about our mission and he seemed very excited. It would be a great opportunity for them, because the tent meeting would draw people to their church and the Holy Spirit would draw people long after we leave the city. Now we had to wait for the Senior Pastor's permission, we would need his "ok" to use the lot. So wait, we did. At the same time, we decided to look for a back-up lot in case the answer was, "no."

As I looked around the campground, I saw so many needs. Some people lived there even though it was supposed to be a temporary campground, many were hurting and broken. The next day was Sunday, May 31st. I arranged to have an outside service under the small pavilion at the campground in the morning, no sense in wasting time.

We headed out to look for a library to upload our journal report to the website and to keep in contact with everyone back home, which we tried to do as much as possible. Unfortunately, we had no phone reception in our campground, therefore no wireless internet access. We drove around to study the layout of the land for our outreach; Prescott was a perfect place for our tent meeting, a booming city and a college town.

At the library, we had the privilege to share with two gang bangers, Cyrus and Ricky, they had tattoos on their necks,

50

and were saggin' and baggin' their pants. They had been drinking and it was only 12 noon. We shared Jesus with them right in the public library; they were both open to the Gospel and prayed to receive Jesus as their Savior. They promised they would come to the tent meeting when it started. Immediately after we finished praying with them, two other teens about 18 years old walked by; one with screaming lime-green hair, the other with bright yellow, color-crayon hair. We gave them a full witness as well, they listened until the young girl with lime green hair said, "I was raised in church, I don't want to listen, I can do what I want to now." She was angry; we shall keep her in prayer.

We headed back to the campground, and I realized once again, there are no coincidences with the Lord. God is amazing; he will go to great lengths to demonstrate His love: the man in the R.V. parked right next to us was named Rex, he looked so broken inside. The more I talked to him, I realized he was a backslider; his mother raised him in the Word. As a young boy of 16, he was thrown out of church after he was caught sleeping with the pastor's wife who was 12 years older than him.

I could see the hurt in his eyes and felt the deep pain as he told his story; he was now 63 years old and has never been back to church. I told him, "Jesus set him next to our campsite for a reason. God's love is never ending!" I shared how the devil set him up and used that woman to seduce him, to steal God's plan for his life. He started to weep; his spirit was so broken inside. I told him, "God loves you Rex! He shook His head, "No, I'm going to hell for what I did, the church hissed at me as they threw me out of the church

51

that day, they had me walk from the altar down the center aisle out the door, hissing at me all the way." He continued, "That was the day I drank my first drink and smoked my first cigarette." He was so self-condemned, the devil thoroughly condemned him and Rex believed the lies. I prayed for him. We had three days next to Rex's motor home before he was scheduled to leave the camp. The Holy Spirit strategically sent us to show the love of Jesus to him once again.

The office manager gave me permission to have the church service, our mission was to reach Willow RV Park. We blanketed the campground with fliers. There were approximately 100 different campsites and we went trailer-to-trailer, tent-to-tent, inviting everyone to church, for the next day's Sunday service. We put out over 200 gospel tracts on this Saturday alone and prayed for salvation with Cyrus and Ricky at the library, praise God!

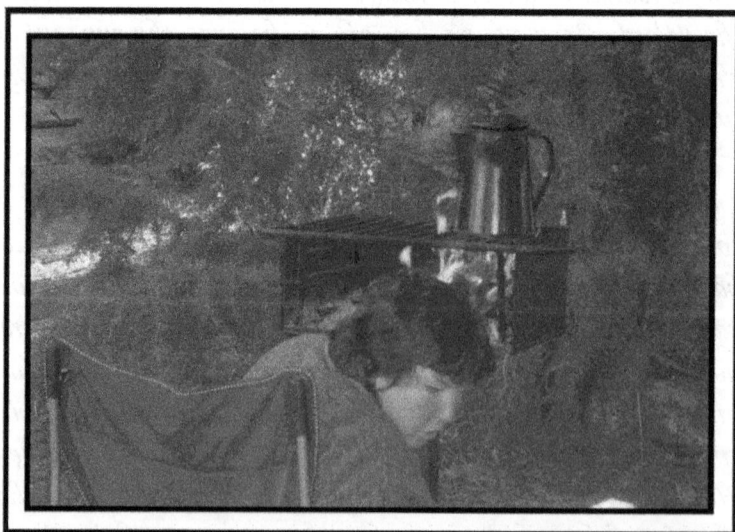

I woke up at 4:45 a.m. again without an alarm. Thanks to Jill, we had coffee every morning. Thank God because the overnight temperature was less than 45 degrees, brrrr! The air leaked out of my air mattress and boy was I cold. I was hoping that maybe after seven days, we would get the hang of this camping thing.

Every one of the team members went into motion, "Lock and Load," as we made ready for service at the Willow RV Park Pavilion. Rhonda and Kaweah dressed in black slacks and our Mission America t-shirts, Rhonda had her keyboard in hand, as they marched to the pavilion and started singing. Wow! The power of the Holy Spirit came pouring down from heaven. Kaweah's voice could be heard throughout the whole park, I could hear her from our tent site, and it sounded like Kaweah and Rhonda were accompanied by angels.

I stood to join them singing worship, the presence of the Holy Spirit fell on that park from above. As we were singing, people were coming with chairs in hand from every direction. About 14 people came to sit down and many more stood and sat afar off through the whole service, they definitely heard the message. The pavilion was right across from the campground's store and laundry mat.

A young lady who had separated herself to the farthest, most remote area of the park as slept in her van, she suddenly came out of her hiding place to walk down the road close to the pavilion, as if marching by on assignment. We noticed her the first day, she would only come out in the dark, Kaweah & I found her in the shower room late at night taking a shower for almost an hour, running the hot water so long the women's restroom became a sauna. I asked her not to waste the water, she completely ignored me. It was interesting for someone who is in absolute isolation and fear to march boldly during the most crowded time and place in the park, a clear indication to me of the invisible battle waging amongst the people there. She was not the only peculiar person we ran into during our stay.

Although, I appreciated every person who joined us, my heart was touched the most by Rex. No, he did not bring a chair or sit down for church. Beverly told me, she watched him as he walked to wash his laundry, she noticed him during the sermon part of the service. With dirty clothes in hand, he stopped in the middle of the road, mesmerized, listening to the Word of God, the Holy Spirit was drawing him back, Jesus was holding open loving arms. After most of the message, it was as if he realized where he was and started walking again to his original destination, the laundry mat.

Finally, I gave an altar call and asked for those who needed healing. I prayed for those who were sick and preached the straight Word of God. As I looked around, a wonderful woman was weeping as the Holy Spirit touched her, what a sweet presence of the Lord. People throughout the whole park heard the Word of God, several others besides Rex, pretended they were checking their laundry, as they stood and listened, held captive by the music and the Word. Jesus used us to bring his presence to set the captives free at the campground.

I looked at the clock, we only had 15 minutes to make it to another church service at the Prescott First Assembly of God because we had a meeting with Pastor Steve, the Senior Pastor. I wanted to meet him in person and ask permission to use his lot, the location was ideal. We made it a few minutes late, found chairs and entered into prayer. The pastor's sermon was about child-like faith – he preached a great message.

After the service was over, we waited around for the pastor to finish speaking to his church members. As a minister, I understood he had to attend to his people first. Finally, after everyone left, Pastor Adam, the youth pastor came to show us his youth church, a very cool setting. I saw first hand the fruit of his spirit through the youth in the church, they were the ones who greeted us warmly and welcomed us in love. I know the Lord has great things ahead for Adam; his position as youth pastor is only the beginning of God's destiny for him.

We met with Pastor Steve, the Senior Pastor, in his office. The first thing he asked for was my references. On one hand, I understood because he did not know me at all. At the same time, I thought to myself, "Funny how Jesus was a man of no reputation, ministering from city-to-city, village-to-village without references." I did not come to Prescott to make a name for myself or to gain personal recognition; I am driven by this sole purpose, to see people rescued out of the depths of darkness, to see lives changed through the saving power of Jesus, Luke 4:18.

After the meeting with Pastor Steve we left the property, he said he needed more time to make his decision. Prescott First Assembly was my first choice, yet I also knew we should keep looking for a back-up lot just in case. Time was so important because our goal was to have our tent up before Wednesday, June 3rd and start our Tent Meeting Thursday, June 4th. We would hold services in the tent every night through Sunday, June 7th. I knew by the Holy Spirit, the city of Prescott, Arizona was a great harvest field, ripe for the gospel.

We stopped by the Goodwill store to get a few items; we did not have, after all we did not pack for cold weather; we didn't think we would need wool socks, a wool hat or winter stuff in Arizona in the summer. Guess who crossed our path again? The precious couple we met a few days earlier in Camp Verde, Ken and Trisha; we told them God must have a GPS there was no other way to schedule these divine appointments otherwise. What are the odds of being in their path five days later in a different city? I would say a long shot. God always has a plan, Ken said he would talk to his pastor about another lot for our tent meeting in case the first one does not come through; they really want to help us out.

We witnessed everywhere we went, passed out gospel tracts every chance we had. A young man named, Joe (Joseph) prayed for salvation that Sunday, he was the cashier at the Goodwill store.

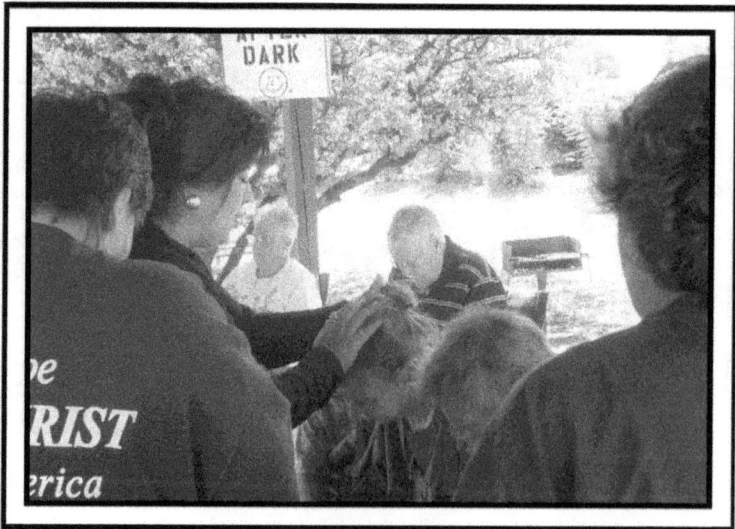

Chapter Seven
Mission America Journey

Modern Day Book of Acts

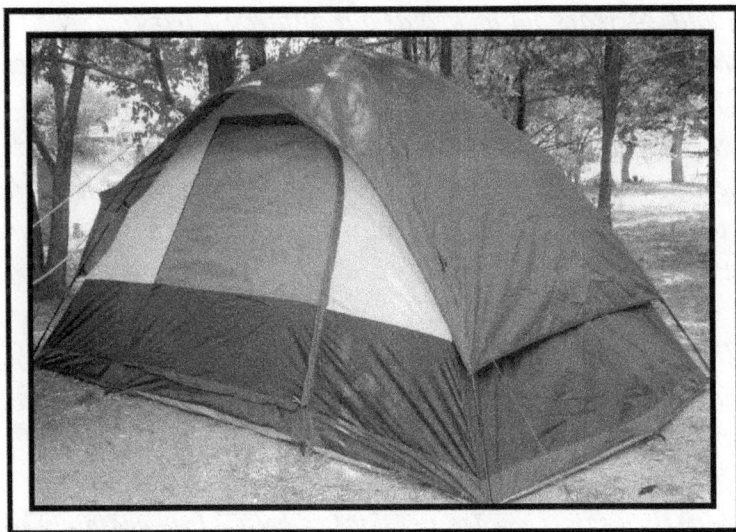

*W*ords alone could not express what I felt deep inside of my heart on this day, Monday, June 1st. What a powerful and wonderful God we serve, He is so loving and so thoughtful.

We started the day at the campground, a bit sore, yet I was definitely warm when I slept. When I opened my tent window, I couldn't resist taking the picture of Jill making sure we had our coffee first thing in the morning she always kept the little fire stoked. I decided we were going to stay in the tents at this campground for the rest of our time here in Prescott, we could do it. The girls' job was to clean up; set the table with a nice tablecloth for our meals; Beverly and I would go to the coffee shop to set up our traveling office and upload reports to the website.

We walked into the coffee shop and started setting up our table, chairs, laptop and printer. A handsome young man about 24 years old looked at our t-shirts; I felt compelled by the Holy Spirit to instantly give him one of the tracts, "Jesus Is Coming, Are You Ready?" He started talking to me immediately, the Lord really stirred my heart and I began to prophesy to him. As I was prophesying over him, every hair on his arm and body was electrified, he said they were standing up.

The young man began to weep; he said, "I can't believe this, this is God. I received the Baptism in the Holy Spirit, speaking in tongues four years ago. I was praying all the time in the Spirit when the people at the church told me to stop, they said I needed psychiatric help." I immediately felt my blood begin to boil. I said, "Young man, God's hand is on your life and God ordained this meeting between you and I at this little coffee shop today." He cried openly and said, "I know God called me to do something more." He said he

60

would come to the tent meeting with his wife, they were on vacation from Phoenix.

You never know who you are going to meet when walking on God's roadmap. It's funny how the familiar sound of a Harley catches my ear every time. I glanced outside the window and to my right, I saw an old Harley, and then I went back to work. We were busy making sure we could get everything uploaded and finished when a towering, tall, distinguished looking gentleman dressed in his biker gear walked into the coffee shop. He had a grey beard, sunglasses; complete with jeans and worn jean jacket. He sat directly across from me, even though there were plenty of other tables and chairs. You know how you know somebody is watching your every move; I wanted to go up and say, "Take off your glasses; you're inside!"

After about 20 minutes, I couldn't handle it, I stood up and said, "Let me come over here and sit for a minute while she finishes up some work," referring to Beverly working on the laptop. He looked at my t-shirt and said, "Don't come over here preaching that junk to me." He was quite rude, and I said, "Excuse me sir, what do you mean junk?" We engaged each other for about 15 minutes. I could tell he was a hard case and a bit feisty, on the other hand, he just met his match. I thought to myself, "I'm not gonna let him just have his way and speak his mind." Putting my hand up, I said, "It's my turn," as he was ranting and raving against Christianity. I said, "By the way, what's your name?" He said, "My name's Hawk." He said, "I believe like the Indians do." I said, "As a matter a fact, I am full blooded Apache, I am an Indian. I'm talking about the great God, the Almighty God, the only All Knowing God, I'm not talking about the little "g" gods!" I think I got his attention. He stared at me eye-to-eye and I stared right back through those sunglasses.

I knew he was a special man, if I could get him out of being ornery long enough to hear the truth; God just might make a preacher out of him. Then I discovered he was a character actor who played in many movies and TV programs; most of them westerns. He had his faithful coffee cup with pictures of himself beside Grizzly Adams, Michael Landon; etc. Guess what? Before we packed up and left, he said he would come to the tent meeting, too.

It was Monday and the call came from Pastor Steve, his answer was "Yes," we now had permission to set up our tent on the church lot. At almost the exact same moment, we received a phone call from a wonderful lady named Linda Riley along with her husband Jay, they said they wanted to take us in.

On Saturday when we were at the library, Jill logged onto the internet and was searching for housing options; she found several on craigslist and came upon the Blessing Retreat Bed & Breakfast. She had Beverly call and talk to Linda, Beverly told her we had four missionary puppies. Linda regretfully said she could not help us because she was expecting other guests and with the quality of accommodations, she could not take dogs. As Jill prayed over the weekend, the Holy Spirit must have spoken to Linda because on Sunday, she sent her husband Jay and a friend out driving to all the campgrounds trying to find us.

They could not get through to us by phone because we were in a "dead" zone at the Willow RV Park. Kaweah and Rhonda came to find us at the coffee shop, when the cell service kicked on; Linda's phone message was received on Kaweah's phone. Kaweah gave me the message right away because Linda wanted me to call back. I could only stand back and watch the hand of the Lord, our Provider at work.

> **_Acts 16:14-15_**, "Now a certain woman named Lydia heard us. She was a seller of purple from the city of Thyatira, who worshiped God. The Lord opened her heart to heed the things spoken by Paul. And when she and her household were baptized, she begged us, saying, 'If you have judged me to be faithful to the Lord, come to my house and stay. So she persuaded us.'"

The same day we received news of the lot approval, we were also invited to stay at the best Bed & Breakfast in the city, Blessing Retreat. Since we did not know the area, we started our drive to the Riley's home. As I looked around I knew we were in a high end area, just by looking at the type of surrounding properties, I would say million dollar plus homes.

When we reached the house we were speechless; the home was right out of the Home & Garden Magazine; a beautiful, white Victorian style home with a wrap around porch. As I stepped out of the car, I double-checked with Beverly, "Are you sure she knows we have dogs?"

63

The door opened, and out came an incredible woman. She welcomed us as if we were family; hugging us, and saying, "I have homemade chocolate chip cookies, tea, and lemonade set out before I show you your rooms." She was very hospitable and at the same time firm when she gave us the rules, "Wash your hands when you come into the house and a few others," we were more than glad to oblige. We walked into her beautiful white kitchen complete with white tile floors, waxed, solid oak floors everywhere else, and everything was so neat and orderly. Looking around I smiled, she loved antiques, and we had a similar liking for interior design.

All of us sat down at the kitchen table when her husband, Jay walked in. He had such a sweet spirit. He had a long grey beard and long gray curly hair down to the middle of his back. "There is something special about this man," I thought. He sat with us, smiled and had a twinkle in his blue eyes when he asked about our mission. I felt like I was in the presence of Elijah, his spirit was not only sweet, but gentle as well. I discerned by the Holy Spirit that this man had loved the Lord for a long time and had been His servant. Later on I discovered he had been a pastor for over 30 years. What fellowship we had with him and his lovely wife. We shared about Mission America and I could tell they were both touched and moved with compassion for the lost souls of men and women.

Jay & Linda Riley
Blessing Retreat Bed & Breakfast

How can I describe how they welcomed us? No words can correctly express the great kindness and generosity they showed all of us. They opened up not just their home, for the whole week of our meetings; they also served us breakfast every morning at 7:30 am. I cannot begin to describe to you the royal treatment we received at the home of Jay and Linda Riley, Please always pray for a super blessing on this couple.

Did I forget to tell you Linda is a writer? Her book is amazing, titled, "The Call to Love," her book should be read by everyone, she not only told personal stories but she walks *in the Master's Love; what a true example of the love of Christ!*

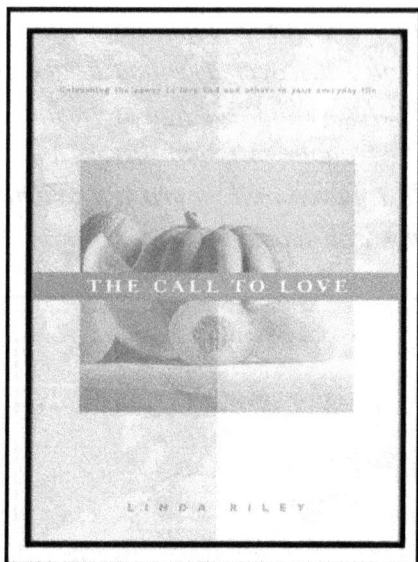

Can be ordered on our website
www.atouchfromabove.org

Do you think Jesus loves what we are doing? I think so! He knew, whether cold or hot, campground or not, we would be faithful to do His work. Our Jesus loved us so much; He prepared the very best in Prescott, Arizona. I am humbled and honored to have been in this home. I am a daughter of the King staying in a King's Home!

Chapter Eight
Mission America Journey

Let the Work Begin

I woke up at 5:00 am on Tuesday, June 2nd. Breakfast
was served at 7:30 am afterwards we joined Pastor
Jay and Linda for an hour of praise and prayer in the
enormous living room. The presence of the Holy Spirit was

truly there as promised in Matthew 18:20, "For where two or three are gathered together in My name, I am there in the midst of them." It truly was a Book of Acts meeting at the Blessing Retreat that morning; we shared communion together and a prophetic Word from the Lord. The day before, Beverly received a message from the Holy Spirit from Joshua 6, specifically verse 16, "Shout, for the Lord has given you the city!" The purpose of God's message, to our team, pastors in Prescott and other believers was to confirm and encourage us, as he did Joshua's army in their battle for the city of Jericho. The Lord reconfirmed His message before we left town, I will explain later in the book.

When our group devotions were over, Linda invited us to stay at the Blessing Retreat for the whole time we were in Prescott. I looked at my daughter, Kaweah, tears filled her eyes because she was deeply touched by our Heavenly Father's goodness to us. We all knew this was a remarkable answer to prayer and a magnificent blessing. Originally, when Linda asked us to stay, she had tentative reservations from paying customers; she offered us a few days free of charge.

After all, this was June and the busy season for the Bed & Breakfast industry. I did not say a word to the girls, I just prayed, we were all pleasantly surprised by Pastor Jay & Linda's extremely liberal generosity. Now we all could focus on the tent meeting exclusively, not become distracted by nagging questions, "Where are we going to stay? Do we have enough money for lodging?" I cannot describe the great relief not to waste precious time packing and moving, wondering about safety or freezing in tents, Jesus is faithful to answer our prayers before we ask.

Then off we went to set the tent up on the church's property on a main street directly across from a strip mall and Wal-Mart, the tent would be visible by thousands. A group of men from a ministry called "Church on the Street" came to our aid, what a blessing. It took about 7 hours with all of us; it would have taken 15 hours if it had been just us girls. Praise God for strong men of God.

As I was getting to know each one of the men, I could tell some of them were not truly committed to Jesus yet. Since I've had men's homes as part of our ministry for three decades, it was plain to see the Holy Spirit was needed. We worked hard and I thank God for Darryl, Dale, Brian, Joe and the rest of the men who worked so diligently to the end. The tent was up, oh what grace. We laughed together; Jill, Beverly, Rhonda, and Kaweah were smiling from ear to ear, saying to themselves, thank you Jesus!

We finished up the last part of the set up, packing the accessories and cleaning up around the lot area. We were loading the vehicles to leave when one of the guys asked me to please come to the "Church on the Street" service that night, they asked if I would speak. I told them, "I would be honored," and asked, "What time is church?" They answered in one hour; I hurried back to the Blessing Retreat, cleaned up, and ran out the door. Kaweah was right behind me, we were "running and gunning" just as fast as we could; my Bible in one hand and music in Kaweah's. I had so much more I wanted to write each day, but once the battle plan

69

went into full swing, it was difficult to find time for journaling. Thank the Lord; we have included photos to help us tell this wonderful story. Every time I see a picture of the tent in place, I just want to shout, "Yee haw, Praise the Lord!"

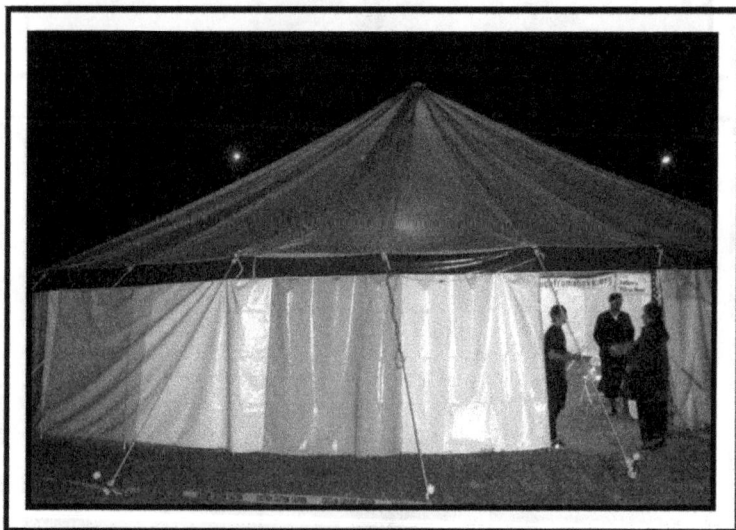

I woke up at 5 a.m. on Wednesday, June 3rd, after a perfect night's rest. The first thing I did was to thank God for the Blessing Retreat and for Pastor Jay and Linda, gifts directly from heaven.

I just wanted to cry, and as you read that statement, please realize I am not just given to crying. These tears came from gratefulness to how much our Heavenly Father loved us, and to spoil His daughters. Also, thankfulness for God's instruments, His special people who He prepared to treat us like royalty because of our willingness to labor and sacrifice for the Great Commission. We were all staying in beautiful rooms and sleeping in comfortable beds, I'm talking about a five star Bed & Breakfast, a wonderful gift from the Lord as we stepped out by faith to do His work. Isn't God amazing? The Spirit of the Lord is able to connect you with others, from another state that have unity in the Spirit, in purpose, and soul winning. We felt right at home as if we had known each other forever. At 7:30 a.m., I heard the call, "Girls, breakfast is ready." What a lovely breakfast, indeed. Linda was truly gifted for hospitality and excellence in B&B meal preparation; those are valuable talents from our amazing God.

We thoroughly enjoyed breakfast again and hurried off, we had a full day ahead of us and the tent meeting started at 7 pm. The "girls", Rhonda, Beverly and Kaweah had to pass out thousands of fliers; not to mention all of the last minute details Jill and I had to attend to. She and I headed to the nearest Home Depot; I had to engineer a way to hang our banner, "Experience the Power of God," on the outside of the tent.

After the girls were done with outreach, Kaweah's next task utilizing her years of ministry training was to set up the inside of the tent. She decorated by hanging each of our small banners and our large American flag for Mission

73

America. While I was finishing up at the tent site, the wind picked up and started blowing hard against the tent. I immediately began to pray, "Lord, please stop the wind." We discovered the winds were unusually strong for June in Prescott; they ended up blowing hard off and on for each day of our tent meeting.

I have always said what is happening in the natural is a parallel of events in the supernatural. As I look back, I am sure the Holy Spirit was blowing the winds of revival through a city which not only experienced a powerful Book of Acts revival in the 1970's during the Jesus people movement. I am not just talking about citywide revival, but the winds of revival blew from the small town of Prescott across the world. Over 30 years later, God gave me and our team the assignment to fan the flames of revival once again. The temptation the enemy brings after every great revival is to suffocate the fire with religion.

I asked the Lord at every stop along the journey, "Why here?" There are various answers in each city and for Prescott, one of them was that our first stop, the beginning of our Mission America tour would start where I started with Christ. The winds of salvation in the 1970s traveled from Prescott, Arizona to Colorado Springs, Colorado where I was drowning in darkness. In February 1979, the Holy Spirit drew me to the cross of Jesus and I gave my life to Christ. In God's providence, He carefully orchestrated the beginning of our mission where I started and brought me full circle by the end of the second tour in October. I found another answer to my question for this location in these verses:

Revelation 3:1-3, *"And to the angel of the church in Sardis write, 'These things says He who has the seven Spirits of God and the seven stars: I know your works, that you have a name that you are alive, but you are dead. Be watchful, and strengthen the things which remain, that are ready to die, for I have not found your works perfect before God. Remember, therefore how you have received and heard; hold fast and repent. Therefore if you will not watch, I will come upon you as a thief, and you will not know what hour I will come upon you."*

Jesus is so fantastic, He loves the people so much He strategically creates battle plans to bring exhortation and repentance so the cold, "dying," religious crowd could find repentance before judgment can destroy them. Even more so, the Good Shepherd does whatever it takes to rescue a new generation of souls, those who have yet to get an opportunity for the life more abundantly in Christ. On top of everything else, God Almighty speaks to me over three decades bringing me into town, *"...on the wings of the wind,"* Psalm 18:10. I am fruit which remained from the original revival, honored and privileged to ignite the fire of revival once again.

Jill and I headed over to the hospital because Linda Riley's mother was admitted earlier in the week; she was 86 years old at the time. Pastor Jay & Linda had been praying for her for over 30 years and I was urged by the Holy Spirit, He clearly spoke to my heart, "Go and close the deal." When I entered her room, I found a stunning, but frail, silver-haired woman lying on the hospital bed. We talked, bonded together for about 35 minutes; then I felt it was time to ask her if I could pray for her healing. I shared about Jesus, how He loved her. She gripped my hand with both of her hands and with tears in her eyes; she repeated the sinner's prayer with such sincerity. The presence of the Lord came into the room so strong, almost like a cloud, she was gloriously saved.

Finally, all the errands were completed and Jill dropped me off at the Blessing Retreat. My next job was to pray for three hours for the opening night. I was so excited and expecting God to do great things. In the meantime, Jill was directing the finishing touches for set up. When she returned to the tent to set up the sound equipment something was wrong. She tried everything she knew, the main speaker was not working.

It was very time consuming; checking each cord trying desperately to trouble shoot the problem in enough time to get dressed and get back to the tent on time. I was waiting for all the girls to return because both vehicles were at the tent location; they were my ride to the meeting. When they did not come back to the house by 6:30 p.m., I knew something was wrong; yet I had no phone reception to check on them. Finally, Jill & Beverly came running through the door to get dressed; I ironed their blouses for them and helped them get ready. We had 10 minutes to get to the tent, we were off.

You know you are doing something right when the wind is howling like crazy, the sound equipment breaks down, and

76

you are running late. We walked into the tent and the worship had already begun, thank the Lord Kaweah & Rhonda got ready early and they were able to stay at the tent site. Despite the hectic activity before our arrival, there was a sweet presence of the Lord in the tent. Some people had arrived over an hour early; some came from the Willow RV park church service the previous Sunday. The people were hungry for a touch from the Lord.

I preached a message about how you cannot live in two worlds and the parable of the ten virgins in Matthew 25:1-13. I asked those who were true Christians to stand to their feet, many were still sitting down and then I called them forward to make a decision for Christ. They willingly stood up from their chairs and walked to the front near the podium, the altar filled up quickly. There was a spirit of true repentance in the tent. Then I prayed for the people who came forward, there were so many I had to ask Pastor Jay and a few other ministers in the tent to help me pray for the people at the altar, we were all busy.

An incredible lady named Kathy Stanton came forward to receive the baptism of the Holy Spirit; she was a friend of Linda's. The sweet presence of the Lord touched her and she began to speak in tongues, a special and powerful event, she received her own personal prayer language. She really began to tear up, the Lord was renewing and restoring a new walk in her; she had been sick for a long time, she is so precious. God really moved during the opening night of the tent meeting; so many were healed, saved, and touched by the Holy Spirit. I could not have asked for anything more, our

God is marvelous. Thank you Jesus for those who prayed for the wind to stop, the blowing ceased at last, praise God.

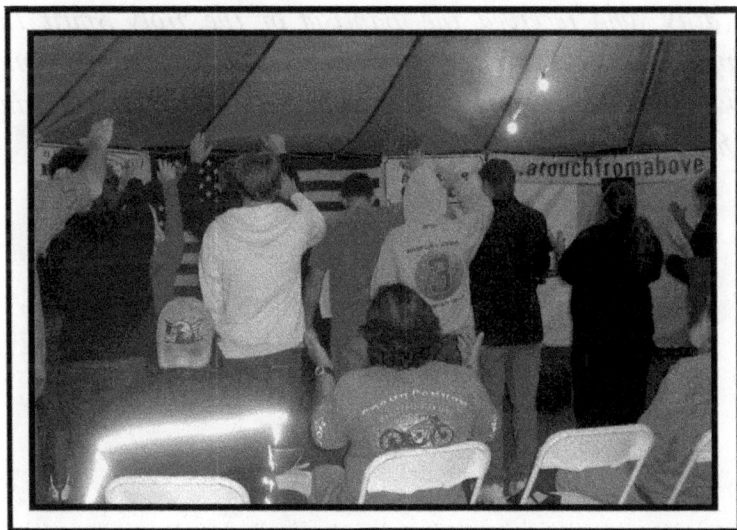

Once again, we were up early for breakfast on Thursday, June 4th. Every morning I awoke at the Blessing Retreat, I knew our stay there was a special treat from the Lord,

especially the value of the peace of God which dominated the entirety of the home. There was a dedicated prayer room, thus peace prevailed, Philippians 4:6-8.

We were full of energy and ready to go for the second day of our mission in Prescott. The team took out thousands of fliers and I had 3½ hours to pray, what a joy. By the afternoon, the wind was howling again at the Blessing Retreat. I looked out my window and the trees were waving frantically in the wind. I thought, "Oh Lord, have mercy, please, You calmed the wind last night, I know you can do it again."

Then I heard Linda call out, "Dr. Luauna, somebody's here to see you." At the door stood the precious woman, named Kathy who received the Baptism of the Holy Spirit the night before. She had five beautiful, brand new, sleeping bags with her; she smiled and said, "I thought I would bring these to you in case you ever go to Colorado."

Kathy Stanton

Funny, I had just been praying about Colorado, I wonder what that means. I keep saying, "I'm on my way to Atlanta," no telling what God has planned. I smiled, thanked her, and gave her a great, big hug. I told her, "You're going to make sure we don't freeze, huh?" She was leaving that afternoon to Phoenix, I knew I wouldn't see her again, I ran up the winding staircase to my room to get my camera, I wanted a picture of Kathy Stanton, she is so precious. She told me she was washing dishes this morning and singing in the Holy Spirit, which is only the beginning of what God's going to do in her life.

The girls came back early at 2:00 pm; I wanted them to rest so they would be refreshed for the night. They all left at 4 pm and Jill returned for me at 6 pm. When I arrived at the tent; I said, "Oh Jesus, have mercy." The wind was so strong and some of the poles were moved right out of their position. No matter what we tried, they kept moving. I stood outside, looked up at the top of the tent, I was afraid; it looked like a gigantic sail waving in the wind. It was only the grace of God and those ropes tied to the stakes that kept the tent in place. I went back inside to pray, "Wind be still, in Jesus name."

I looked up to the center of the big pole of the tent and I could see it moving from side-to-side; I was trying hard not to think a million doubts. At one point, the devil even told me, "Maybe you should cancel." I could tell everyone was a little nervous. The devil hates what we're doing, but God is in love with us. I knew we had prayer cover and I started praying for God to send thousands of angels to protect us. As we got started, "BAM," the sound went out. Jill and Beverly worked diligently to find out where the problem was. I knew it was the devil, the wind howling and the tent felt like it was ready for take off at any moment. The entire tent was flapping in the wind; the tent poles were being pulled, moved and shifted. Now our sound equipment broke down.

I said, "This is a job for the Holy Ghost!" I stood up, went forward and said, "Let's just praise God, who needs music?" We just started praising God and I didn't stop, "Come on praise God," we continued praising even though the wind kicked up off and on through the whole service. The second night there seemed to be quite a bit of chaos and distraction. I noticed people were so unsettled, I knew it was demonic. In spite of it all, I preached about Satan, oh, maybe that's why he was so upset. A devil exposed is a devil defeated.

By the end of the night the power of God came down and the tent stayed up. The altar was filled with people repenting and wanting healing from the Lord. This second night seemed as if we were battling with a lot of demonic, religious spirits, I could feel the forces of darkness. Religion is a strange thing; it has no concern for salvation, healing, and the redemption of others. In spite of it all, people were saved, and touched by God's wonderful Spirit.

On the third night, Friday, June 5th, we took hold of the demonic forces and put them under our feet in the name of Jesus. Each night we were increasing in attendance and we had two more nights to go. Thank you to all those who remembered to pray for us, the best days were ahead for this tent revival. Some of the locals told me, this is strange weather for Prescott in June. I was confident in my Lord; He is in control, even of the winds and the weather, Amen.

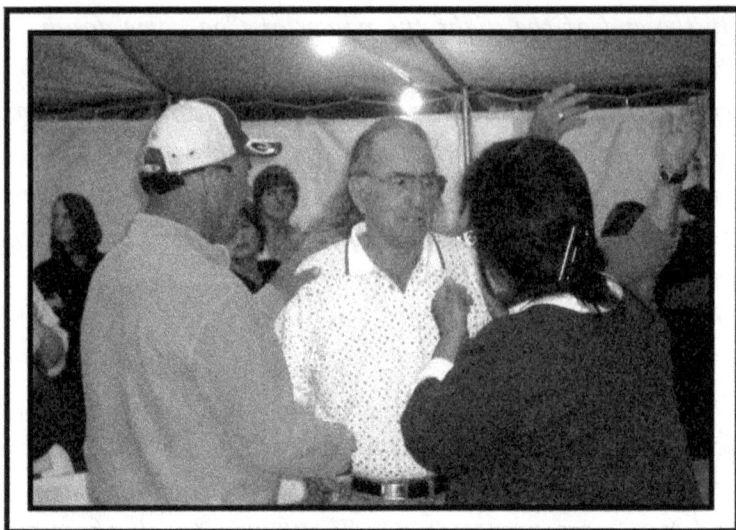

Chapter Nine
Mission America Journey

Lives Touched Forever

*W*e started on the road gain heading towards Atlanta, Georgia on Tuesday, June 9th. As I was leaving Prescott, thinking how sorry I was because I did not have time to write in my journal everyday. We were so busy, good, productive busy laboring in God's kingdom. It was like one day ran right into another; at the same time I was so excited about everything God did with our time in Prescott, Arizona.

The five day tent meeting was a great success. How does one measure success? Religion always wants to measure success by numbers; we did have a good number of people saved and a fantastic percentage of true repentance. Almost every person who walked into the tent was hungry for a touch from the Lord, we had over 60 people in the tent every service, and attendance increased every night.

This was all done to the glory and power of God, the Master Craftsman of A Touch From Above Mission America. Think about this, five single women, four missionary "doggies," one Toyota truck pulling a 6' foot trailer and a second vehicle holding passengers, puppies, and luggage. A trailer filled with a 50' round revival tent, 250,000 gospel tracts, folding chairs, sound equipment, and luggage. A missionary team embarking on a road trip on an evangelistic mission with no advance destinations, contacts, or schedule with a finite amount of money to fund the trip.

When we left town after 12 days, we had the most perfect tent location, established a network of contacts with Prescott First Assembly, Hope Chapel Foursquare Church, Prescott Healing Rooms and Church on the Street Men's Home ministry; not to mention working with a network of local believers from all different churches to bring in a harvest of souls.

Then there were the vendors who donated vital services: Steve Large owner of Buckaroo's Potties & Septics, LLC who provided the portable toilet (in his time of grief for his young wife, he generously gave to us); Bruce & Nancy Montroy owners of Banners & More printed the tent meeting information on our fliers which we were printed by Mark & Suzanne Olsiewski owners of Impressions-In-Ink in San Diego; and of course, Pastor Jay & Linda Riley owners of Blessing Retreat Bed and Breakfast.

I realized when we step out in faith, I just stand back and watch the hand of God move. Our greatest measure of success was by establishing God's dominion in the city through our truck and trailer; by declaring God's Word, the hope of Jesus Christ; and through our personal witness to over five thousand people in the Tri-Cities of Prescott, Prescott Valley, and Chino Valley; lifting up the ministers of the local churches and encouraging them to fight the fight of faith for their city. What value can you put on each persons life? Jesus came to visit us every service that is true success.

Many people came to the tent meeting who were not going to church anymore, still searching for answers for their life. Some sick came with oxygen machines and in wheelchairs seeking their miracle healing. Teenagers marked with tattoos on their necks, forearms, and piercings all over their bodies, drawn by the tent and the Holy Spirit. One young man had tattoos throughout his body like a roadmap. You just knew Jesus was needed in this place. Did I forget to mention withstanding over 40 mile an hour winds, every night until the last night when they ceased, and the unusually cold temperatures for Arizona? Thanks to everyone who prayed us through.

The last two nights of the tent meeting were amazing, Saturday, June 7th, & Sunday, June 8th. The power of God was poured out upon us as in the Book of Acts; His kingdom came on earth as it is in heaven, Matthew 6:10. One of those nights I called Christians forward to the altar for freedom from compromise. I challenged them to make a true stand for Christ, almost everyone went forward. A few lingered in their seats as I looked to the right and saw precious teenagers, weeping as the power of God's Spirit brought them to repentance. Young and old, the altar was *filled. I asked Pastor Jay, who thought he was retired, (but we know like Moses, you are never retired in God's kingdom); to come forward again and help me pray for all the people.*

There was such a sweet presence of the Lord, who can express the wonder of His works? What God does in the heart of man in just a moment at an altar, who can describe? Prophets, preachers, teachers and evangelists are made at that special place and repentance comes when deep hidden sin is revealed by the Holy Spirit. Wow, I am amazed at the goodness, mercy and the grace of my God, Jesus loves people! Thank you Dr. Laurie for dropping the seed in my heart to come to Prescott, what a glorious work the Holy Spirit did.

My heart is always touched when I see strong, mature men weep as they commit their heart to Jesus. Every night people were filled with the Holy Spirit's power and began to speak in other tongues, their heavenly language. They shall never be the same.

The last day and night of the tent meeting, June 8th, was marvelous. I met a Spirit-filled Foursquare Pastor who has a church in Prescott, called Hope Chapel. Pastor Les is a treasure in God's harvest field, he is so humble. I felt in my heart that Beverly should call him again on Sunday. We had already called all the Foursquare Churches in the region a few times; on our way from Flagstaff to Prescott and again once when the tent meeting details were finalized. She asked Pastor Les if I could share about Mission America at his Sunday morning service. He readily welcomed us by telephone. When we arrived at his church and walked in we sat down, some of the people were testifying. He and his wife had such a sweet spirit.

After the testimonies were finished, he said, "Excuse me church," and he stepped out of his pulpit, walked out into the congregation where we were sitting, stretched out his hand and said, "Welcome Dr. Luauna, to you and your team." He received us in the love of Jesus with respect and honor, my heart was touched.

He asked me to come forward and share; and before you knew it, the Holy Ghost took over. I had forgotten my glasses and could not see the scriptures or the clock; thank God for the Holy Spirit. The pastor allowed me to continue on; I felt such urgency to share about the harvest field, the power of the Holy Spirit and our mission. I prayed for everyone, for a double filling of the Holy Spirit and for a true commitment to be soul winners.

Before service was over Pastor Pitts led us all to shout, as Joshua did when the walls of Jericho came down; we shouted for Prescott, this was a God-ordained, appointment from heaven to meet with this wonderful church and Pastor Sunday morning. Do you remember when the Holy Spirit gave us a prophetic message the first Sunday we were here, May 31st? The Lord confirmed the same message at our communion service at the Blessing Retreat and once again with Pastor Les Pitts as we were ending our mission in Prescott. Pastor Pitts invited his whole church to come to the tent meeting for the last service that Sunday evening and said he would be there himself.

I have been a Christian leader, pastor and evangelist for 33 years. To take the step of faith and go on Mission America was an extreme challenge and at times a shocker. My spirit was deeply saddened by the way many ministers are tricked by the enemy to walk in fear and suspicion against other ministers. Pastors pray to the Lord of the harvest to send laborers into the harvest field, Matthew 9:37-38. Then when the Holy Spirit hears their prayers and God dispatches the answer they work against the laborers and reject their efforts. When this happens, through God's grace I have trained myself not to react in the flesh and to intercede for my fellow laborers in God's kingdom. After all, we are on the same team!

Unfortunately, I have observed this more than once on both of our Mission America tours. The ministers who embraced our team's efforts each had these characteristics in common and did not know one another; oneness in the Holy Spirit, walking in unity, humility, the fruits of the Spirit, a consistent prayer life and were baptized in the Holy Ghost with the evidence of speaking in tongues.

Paul the Apostle, declared in the Word of God, how some of his own disciples forsook him, 2 Timothy 4:9-16. My desire is to follow Paul's example and not charge their behavior against them, instead to weep and intercede for them. I am only a servant and am determined to always give honor and respect to co-laborers in the ministry for the purpose of God's kingdom.

I knew I was leaving Prescott and these new believers had to have a church home to grow in. The Lord brought Pastor Jay Riley, who had been a pastor of a church in California for over 30 years. He sat humbly at every tent meeting receiving and wholeheartedly excited about Jesus. He brought people to every service and ministered love to the new believers. After speaking with him, he decided to start a new church at the Blessing Retreat Bed and Breakfast. The Lord also brought Pastor Les Pitts, of Hope Chapel to add new believers to his congregation, a great place for them, he and his wife are naturally gifted as shepherds of God's precious sheep. After only a few hours with them that day, I knew they were overflowing with God's love for others. These new baby Christians will be left in good hands.

__Genesis 12:3-4__, "I will bless those who bless you, and I will curse him who curses you; and in you all the families of the earth shall be blessed."

The Lord's covenant and blessing is assured to everyone who would bless Abraham on his journey. We were truly blessed in Arizona and I cannot thank these special friends enough, below is a list of individuals the Lord used as powerful instruments, I am ever grateful for each one:

- *The men's home from Church on the Street for helping us to set up and take down our tent.*
- *Evelyn & Jim for providing delicious meals, and donating sound equipment*
- *The beautiful little Caitlin Davis, 17 years old, who got saved the first night and helped us every night,*

two hours before the service and stayed after until we were finished. And the last day met with us at 6 a.m. to take the tent down. Had it not been for her, bringing us an extra generator, we might not have had lights.

- *Kathy Stanton, the precious lady who received the baptism of the Holy Spirit the first night and bought us five brand new sleeping bags for our trip.*
- *And all those who attended the tent meetings and a special thanks to those who gave financially to Mission America to get us to our next city.*
- *Jay & Linda Riley, who opened their Bed & Breakfast, Blessing Retreat. We will forever be grateful for their kindness and love. Great is their reward.*

Special thanks to our wonderful Savior, who made Himself known to many and the Holy Spirit who led us to Prescott and who came in His Power!

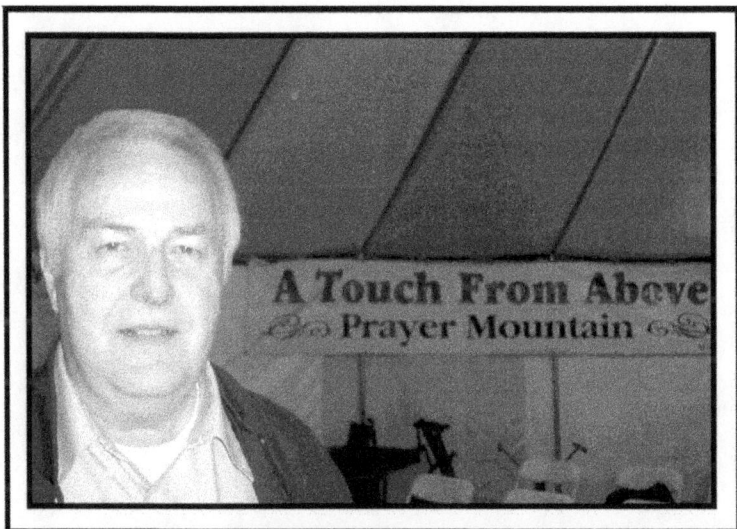

Pastor Les Pitts, Hope Chapel Foursquare Church

Church on the Street

Sydney & Trudy

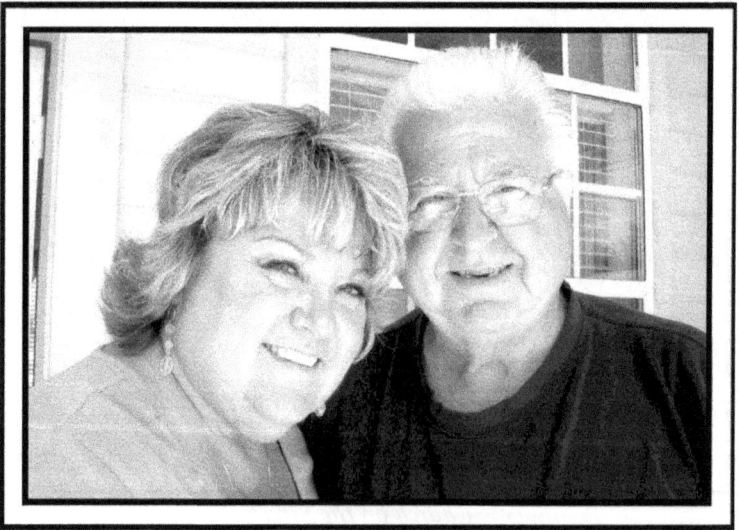

Evelyn & Jim

Chapter Ten
Mission America Journey

Trials & Victories

F rom the moment we left Prescott on Tuesday, June 9th, we were mostly driving and searching for lodging which prevented me from writing in my journal. When we left San Diego we had no idea it would take over 21 days to arrive in Atlanta, we have truly been led by the Holy Spirit. I have been sharing with you the good news and mostly victorious, exciting events; however, we have had our share of trials on this trip, fortunately, we can laugh at some of them.

As I was reminded of Paul, the Apostle's declaration of his suffering for Christ in 2 Corinthians 11:23-33, I understood missionary journeys are not glamorous vacations. The trials I am going to speak of are nothing compared to what he experienced and I would never assume they are equal in comparison, yet they were trials for us nonetheless.

Everyday we had to rely upon our Heavenly Father and pray for finances, gas, food, and lodging all along the way. We pinched pennies as much as possible to stretch the money we did get, trying to keep a budget of $20 a day for five people to eat. I will now give you some highlights from the last few days.

Benson, Arizona, Tuesday, June 9th. We try to stop driving before dark, driving 7-8 hours a day and we made it to Benson, Arizona after we left Prescott. Thank God there was a KOA Campground because you can usually rent an air-conditioned cabin for less than $40 a night; they are dog friendly, and have a laundry area, internet access, showers and grills for cooking. When we drove into Benson KOA, they tried to overcharge us and did not want dogs. We were getting tired and started our search for a motel; I drove into the Super 8, they gave us an excellent price and accepted dogs. When I went to inspect the room; I thought, "Well, we'll be a little bit squashed, but it will work." I did not expect the extra lodgers. I pulled the covers on the bed back, I could not help shouting, "Yuck!" Not only was the sheet filled with someone else's hair, through my peripheral vision, I thought I saw a creepy crawler. Oh my goodness, there was more than one, can someone say, bedbugs?

I immediately, went to the office; tried to be as nice as I could and smiled, after all my t-shirt says, "Jesus," on it. I told the clerk, "I know you are probably not the one who cleans the rooms, but I think someone forgot to clean this room. Do you mind giving us another one?" She turned beet red, and answered, "Wait until I get a hold of the maid." She had excellent customer service and switched our room immediately. There were no bugs, dead or living in sight; except for an occasional cockroach, dead on the sidewalk and tarantulas outside, we were in the desert after all. Super 8 was an excellent choice because the rate included breakfast, so we would eat for free, too.

El Paso, Texas, Wednesday, June 10th, we started investigating whether we could find a KOA or military housing, a few hours closer to our stop time, Rhonda had access to military housing. Nothing could be found; so we decided to try Super 8 again. We found one right off the Interstate in El Paso. By this time we were all hot and tired including the dogs. When I went to the room, it was one-third the size of the room in Benson; talk about a match box. Somehow, they stuffed two double beds with a 12" wide night stand between them, a desk and dresser against the wall. We all just kind of smiled at each other. It was too late to keep driving. We stuffed five women and four dogs into the motel room. The temperature in El Paso that evening was around 100 degrees. Praise the Lord!

After we started winding down, I noticed a bug on the pillow; "Oh, no, not again." It was too late, we were not budging, and we had already unpacked and set up. It took lots of time, energy and skill in the tiny quarters; we would just suffer through this time. I said, "Everyone close your suitcase." Everybody ran for towels to wrap their heads and Beverly started itching. I said, "Beverly you just got here, stop itching wait until tomorrow." Suddenly, Jill was itching. I put my socks on and they asked, "What you are doing?" I said, "I don't want bed bugs between my toes." If I could have jumped in a plastic baggy I would have. We

97

pulled out the air mattresses, some slept on the floor and others in the bed (with bugs), and Kaweah slept underneath the sink, Rhonda slept underneath the desk by the door. We were all packed like sardines into this tiny room. On top of everything else the air conditioner was not working correctly.

Have you ever been to the zoo? Did you notice those little monkeys searching through their friends fur for tiny bugs? The next morning we were doing a bed bug check. One trial on this trip has been not getting a good night sleep, except for our stay at the Blessing Retreat Bed and Breakfast. This has not been easy for anyone except for Beverly who could sleep on concrete.

Midland, Texas, Thursday, June 11th. We were trying to make it to the Abilene, Texas KOA; but I felt "checked" in my spirit. We had over 200 miles to go, it was hot and we were getting tired. Beverly started searching for other campgrounds, military housing and motels. Guess what? Nothing! Even the Super 8, Motel 6 and every motel were completely booked; there was no lodging for miles. I told Beverly to start calling the local Foursquare Churches. The first one she called was Living Way Church, she spoke with Pastor Gary, the youth pastor and explained about our mission and how we could not find a place to stay; he transferred her to the senior pastor, Pastor Jon Wymore. Pastor Jon did not hesitate at all; he received us warmly and gave us directions to the church.

When I met him, I thought he was the youth pastor, because he looked so young; he was only 34 years old at the time and his beautiful wife Pastor Ashley was only 24 years old. They were so sweet and filled with the love of the Lord, they let us sleep in their air conditioned, nursery rooms. Praise God! We enjoyed the fellowship with this special couple; Pastor Jon shared how he just taught out of 3 John two nights before we called:

> **3 John verses 5:8**, "Beloved, you do faithfully whatever you do for the brethren and for strangers, who have borne witness of your love before the church. If you send them forward on their journey in a manner worthy of God, you will do well, because they went forth for His name's sake, taking nothing from the Gentiles. We therefore ought to receive such, that we may become fellow workers for the truth."

When we called, he had an opportunity to put the Word of God into practice.

The trial for this day was the heat. Thank God for the Holy Spirit, the following day we discovered, had we not stopped we would have run right into two tornadoes and flooding. God is good, thank you Jesus for Pastor Jon and Pastor Ashley Wymore and the Living Way Church in Midland, Texas.

Dallas-Fort Worth, Texas, June 5th. We stopped for gas in a little tiny town in Texas, we were getting hungry when an elderly couple saw our trailer, they came up to us and said, they were so touched by what we were doing. The gentleman was 75 years old, he said, "I just told my wife this morning, if God doesn't do something, America is in trouble. We don't have much money, here is $20." He bought our lunch that day, we split sub sandwiches. The Lord has been taking care of us like that since we left San Diego.

After about six hours on the road, Beverly thought about her aunt who lived near Dallas, I remembered meeting Margie (Margaret) at Beverly's dad's funeral. She was not more than 20 minutes off of our route, "Yahoo," she called Beverly back and said she would love to have us stay. She and her husband blessed us tremendously. We were very thankful for the air conditioning, especially and they allowed us to catch up on our laundry, have hot showers, nice sleeping rooms, they fed us dinner and home cooked breakfast, including fresh handmade tortillas. We discovered the wonderful talent of Beverly's uncle; who is an artist, his specialty is in oils. He painted just for fun; I thought to myself, "Get those paintings in a gallery!" I shared some ideas with him and he gave me some tips, because I love to paint as well. Marcelino truly is gifted; I'm sure his paintings would take care of them financially; she would not have to work at Wal-Mart, she could retire at a young age and enjoy herself.

While we were getting ready to leave after doing three loads of laundry, having a full breakfast and basking in the air conditioning; we knew we had to pry ourselves away and get back on the road. The Trevino's were so kind they even allowed our four missionary puppies to stay indoors because of the heat and they normally do not allow dogs in the house. They were so gracious, I think our little Leah, the mother of the herd, sensed love and acceptance she tried to stay there; she never warms up to anyone. Her husband, Tiger is more loyal, we accidentally left him in the dog crate on the porch, as we were walking to the car, he communicated the only way he can, he started barking up a storm, which he normally never does.

Thank God they opened the door for us that night; we would have been in tents in an unbelievable lightning and rain storm. Beverly asked her aunt, "Do you have any sandwich baggies?" Tia Margie asked, "What for?" Beverly smiled from ear-to-ear when she said, "Tortillas." Her aunt woke up early that morning and made a large stack of homemade tortillas. Beverly came out of the kitchen smiling real big, holding several baggies in her hands and said, "Three tortillas for a $1." I'm sure Tia Margie was pleased as Beverly loaded up the tortillas in her bag. We didn't realize the stop before, Beverly loaded up little cubes of butter and jelly; God was preparing for our next days breakfast.

Did I forget to tell you about several semi-truck drivers who almost ran me off the road in hectic Dallas/Fort Worth interstate traffic? A few guys were showing their IQ as they waved their hand at me, also. I'm telling you, there is just something about the name of Jesus, they either love ya or hate ya! The only trial was driving the interstates in Dallas/Fort Worth to get back to our destination; there are over 6.5 million people in the metro area.

Monroe, LA, Saturday, June 13th. We started on the road later than normal when we left Dallas. I knew we needed

101

to find a place to stay and fast, it is always better to set up your tent in the daylight rather than in the dark. Oh-oh, no motels at a reasonable price, I told Beverly look for campgrounds. Beverly went to work, and said; "I found one, Shiloh RV Resort," she was able to research lodging, gas, and many other points of interest with Dr. Laurie's gift, the GPS.

Beverly thought the Shiloh RV Resort sounded good, after all Shiloh appears in several books of the Bible. All the other campgrounds in the area were booked, except for this one. I could see why this one was not booked. First of all, it was almost 100 degrees and the same amount of humidity. All of us looked like little wet rags including the missionary puppies.

As we drove to our Shiloh Resort, I saw some nice, big church buildings with meticulously, manicured landscaping including luscious green grass. I thought to myself, let's just go there and park at their doorstep, but I figured, we better get to the "resort" because at least they had showers.

The girls immediately started setting up our tents, Rhonda, Kaweah and Nala, Kaweah's puppy would share the two-man tent. Jill, Beverly and I along with the other three doggies, Tiger, Leah and Rachel would share the larger tent. We made the tents as comfortable as possible with air mattresses and sleeping bags. In this location, we had to make and keep the screen doors zipped, the mosquitoes were huge. We picked our tent site near the body of water at the edge of the campground, since we came from California, we did not realize it was not a lake, it was a swamp. Can anybody say, "Alligators?" Eeks! We decided, we were not going to complain, we were going to rejoice.

We realized we were out of drinking water. I realized we could not go 20 days and only have eight good nights of sleep. I had to find some kind of foam or something to add to my air mattress. I am not a city slicker who cannot tent camp. I love camping and I am a survivalist. The issues were aches from driving for 6-8 hours each day and many years ago I was in a terrible car accident, and I knew the foam would help me sleep better.

Jill & I back tracked to the store. I saw a few vehicles at the Evangel Temple Assembly of God. We both looked at each other and I said, "To everything God has a purpose, let's stop." The only problem was we looked like homeless, sweaty bums. How was I going to walk in and say, "Hello, I'm Dr. Luauna." Well, I looked in the mirror, and said, "This is going to have to work, I'm in trouble, I never entered a church looking this bad. I prayed, Holy Spirit, please give us favor."

Jill rang the bell to the office and started to return to the car after there was no answer. Suddenly, the door opened and there was a young gentleman standing there, he looked at us as he said, "Uh, hello." I jumped out of the car and said "My name is Dr. Luauna," I put out my hand immediately. We started to talk, but the air conditioner noise outside was so loud, the young man said, "Come on into my office." I replied, "Oh, air conditioning." He looked back and smiled at me, saw the sweat on my forehead and knew I didn't have that Louisiana accent, he knew I was not from their neck of the woods.

As we sat down in his office, he looked at me and said, "Yes," basically asking what I wanted. I knew right then, I had about three minutes to convince him we weren't homeless. He asked me for letterhead as proof that our ministry was valid. I noticed his laptop sitting right in front of him and I said, "Sir, do you have the internet? Let me just take you to our website, I don't have any letterhead on me right now." I immediately took him to the website and shared our mission. Pastor James was his name, he was the assistant pastor. I knew God was doing something special right then and there.

He said, "Give me your number." The funny thing is my phone was dead for several days and I almost forgot Beverly's phone number, I was so tired it was the end of the day. I finally remembered and gave Pastor James the number. He said he was going to talk to the Senior Pastor. At that moment, I decided, I might as well be bold, the words just came out of my mouth, "I'd like to have an opportunity to share our mission at your Sunday service tomorrow morning." I said, "God bless you, thank you for your time Pastor James," and Jill & I left the building.

When we returned to the campground, the Senior Pastor, Calvin Stapp had called Beverly. He asked her about Dr. Cho, because he saw the pictures of Dr. Cho on our website and wanted to know if I was affiliated with the Assemblies of God. He said he was going to pray about giving me 10 minutes to share the next day or allow me to minister for the whole service. That night we prayed and thanked God for favor, then got ready to sleep.

It was hot and humid; the temperature never cooled down at all. In the middle of the night, two of the dogs needed to be walked, Jill and Beverly took them and were eaten alive by mosquitoes from the ankles down, some bites on the arms, and I am talking about some real, big swamp-sized mosquitoes.

I set my alarm and we all were up early in the morning because we had to pack the camp and load everything on top of getting dressed up for church. I didn't know if we were getting 10 minutes or the whole service, we just knew God was going to do something. When we arrived at the church, there was such a sweet spirit from both the assistant, Pastor James and the Senior Pastor, Calvin Stapp.

Pastor Calvin just smiled as Beverly told him about our dogs, she asked, if they had a room for them because they are kennel trained and we could not leave them in the car and it was too hot to leave them in the back of the truck. Pastor Calvin said, "Bring them right into my office." What a godly welcome he gave us; he was filled with God's love, compassion and kindness. Later we met several other people from his church; they all had the same spirit. What a joy to be in Evangel Temple Assembly of God church.

After praise and worship time, Pastor Calvin took the pulpit and ministered for about 15 minutes, I could almost see the Holy Spirit speaking to him, he seemed like he was *going to continue preaching when all of the sudden he called me forward to finish off the service.*

I challenged the church to win the lost and reach souls for Christ. I exhorted them to go out into the harvest field. This precious church was filled with faithful, older people who I knew had experienced revival in this country before. I finished with an altar call, "Who will make a stand, who will win a lost soul?" I called whomever the Holy Spirit was speaking to come forward. The altar was packed. As I began to lay hands on each one for the power of the Holy Ghost, God's presence was so strong. The Lord was stirring up a new fire and a new zeal in the hearts of His people.

As I prayed for every single person and got to the end of the altar, I noticed a very distinguished gentleman in a black suit, with silver-gray hair, weeping in the humility of God, praying in the Spirit. As I reached my hand out to pray for him, I sensed the Holy Spirit speaking to my heart, "This is a mighty man of valor." I reached for him and asked him to please stand to his feet and pray for the gentleman that stood before him, what a powerful man.

Later, I discovered he was 90 years old at the time; he served in ministry for over 70 years and was the Superintendent of the Assemblies of God for the state of Louisiana for 50 years, Mr. Lowell Ashbrook. He is truly a General of the Faith, I knew I wanted this man to anoint me with oil and pray for me. He prayed for God's favor, blessing, and health and for every need to be met. As he looked at me with those godly, piercing blue eyes, he said, "I'm proud of what you are doing, keep up the good work,

106

you blessed us today." I felt as if I was in the presence of Samuel the prophet.

At the end of the service, Pastor Stapp stood up and said to his congregation, "The Lord brought this lady to encourage and challenge us. Go back to the table and bless her ministry." Thank God for a man of God who welcomes servants of the Lord, this was truly a privilege and another Divine appointment!

I understood before we left San Diego I would come in contact with churches and ministries along the way; some would receive us and some would not. I further understood we were strangers, pastors did not know who we were, yet some received us in the unity of the Spirit with the bond of peace. We prayed for the Lord to prepare such Christians and ministers along the way, just as when Jesus sent out the twelve disciples, Matthew 10:5-12.

Our only goal is to win souls, encourage local churches and build up the Kingdom of God in the United States of America on Mission America Tours 1 & 2. I know God will bring a great blessing upon those who receive us because when we leave, we leave a multitude of souls in their care.

I am amazed as I pondered how my travels around the world took me to Africa, Europe, Canada, Mexico and South Korea and I was received in the name of the Lord as well, Matthew 10:40-42. Dr. Cho, the pastor of the largest Christian church in the world, Yoido Full Gospel Church in Seoul, South Korea, received me and my whole team into his office more than once, without any reservation. He truly is a humble man of God; which explains why the Lord has trusted him to build the largest church in the world. He has received a prophet's reward because of his great love for God and love for God's servants; a sure formula to destroy the snare of fear and suspicion set by the devil against ministers worldwide. I do not say this to point the finger, but as a reminder for our team to treat others in the same fashion when they come to us in San Diego and at our Prayer Mountain. Lord, please help us.

This road trip has shown me the pulse of American Christianity, which is being suffocated by the plague of religion. Who is the author of this destruction? It is not the pastors or ministers, we are wrestling against unseen forces. Fear, unbelief, and suspicion are not words in God's vocabulary, these words are not part of the Lord's training manual for Christian leadership, nor should they describe Christian behavior. We called over 50 different churches since we have been on the road, I could write a book alone on the response from those calls, but instead I will write about faith and victory. I will continue to weep between the porch and the altar for my fellow laborers in God's kingdom.

I will say this, one of those calls still makes me laugh, I will not tell you which city or even the name of the church; but when I heard they needed to talk to legal counsel before they could receive us, I wanted to laugh. Instead of feeling rejected, the Holy Spirit encouraged me that Jesus Christ, his disciples, and the Apostle Paul experienced the same thing in Biblical times. Ok, we have not been physically persecuted as they were. Every person who has stepped out *to fulfill the Great Commission throughout history and around the world have been rejected, I would say we are in good company and I never want to make anyone feel rejected. Jesus answered his disciples in Matthew 1-4, when they asked him who was the greatest in the kingdom of heaven, his answer was those with child-like humility.*

It is terrible to feel like you have to drop names and credentials to be accepted. I learned so much on this journey. I will prepare, Lord willing, a beautiful missionary cabin on the Prayer Mountain and when the brethren or sisters come from around the world, I will welcome them with open arms.

As of June 15th, after 22 days on the road we recorded 100 prayers of salvation, distributed over 7,000 gospel tracts and it was just the beginning. We finally arrived in Atlanta, Georgia, now our work really begins!

Beverly, Aunt Margie & Uncle Marcelino

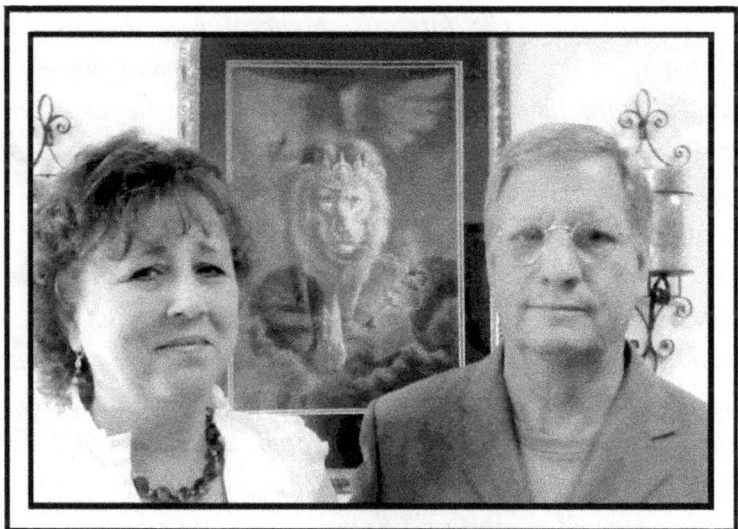

Pastor Calvin & Mrs. Stapp

Chapter Eleven
Mission America Journey,

Atlanta: We Made It!

We arrived in Atlanta, Georgia on Monday, June 15th, in the late afternoon. The first night we stayed with my son, Sam Stines. He had a small house but he welcomed us with open arms. We knew we could not stay there more than one night; five women, husband and wife, three children and four dogs.

On Tuesday, June 16th, after a good nights sleep at Sam's place we began our search for lodging. Beverly had already submitted requests for housing before we arrived in the city, we asked for lodging for five missionary women needing a place for possibly a week or maybe two. We had four responses right off the bat and we were praising God. One man contacted us and said he would allow us to stay in his empty rental for a week for two for free, we made the appointment for Marietta and punched the address in the GPS. Jill, Beverly and I were headed to the interview when he called and said we would have to pay $100 a week for utilities. We could not afford that so we thanked him and declined.

We decided to check about the response we received from a homeowner in Alpharetta, it seemed to be in a safe neighborhood and the gentleman was a Christian. He was a single man who normally rented out his basement, but since it was empty he offered it to us for free. On the telephone he originally said he would offer the accommodations for a few days only. That could be a setback since if we did stay there then in a few days, we would be on the hunt again and would have to take time out to pack and move.

We followed the directions on the GPS and we entered a gated community, which included beautiful homes with large wooded yards and complete with it's own lake, swimming facilities, and so much more. The man's name is Craig; his basement was a large, complete two bedroom apartment with a separate entrance including full bathroom, living room, kitchen and use of his washer and dryer for our laundry. When we met Craig, he was very quiet; Beverly said he was a man of few words on the telephone as well.

Due to different interaction with him through emails, phone calls, and his quiet matter-of-fact attitude, I told Beverly, he is probably an engineer. I have met many engineers who are brilliant and shy at the same time. He came outside to greet us as we drove into his driveway. Bingo! I could tell immediately, he was an intelligent man. He took us through the basement, gave us some ground rules. I had to giggle inside for I knew we were not partiers, drinkers, smokers, and we "don't chew nor go with boys that do". Of course, he didn't know us and as we began to talk I could see his walls came down. We liked the place and it was only 15 minutes from my son's home, and 45 minutes from downtown Atlanta.

The great benefit as missionaries to America while we are in Atlanta, I had the blessing of being able to see my son, his wife and his children, while we are laboring for the Lord. The apartment needed just a little bit of cleaning and we needed to get settled. We moved in that Tuesday, June 16*h*.

Have you ever seen the old western movies which had vagabonds who carry their clothes wrapped on top of a stick in handkerchief, they were homeless going from place-to-place? I prayed, "Lord I don't want to feel like a little vagabond and I don't want to move from house-to-house, we need a place for the whole three weeks." Another gentleman called and offered us a place for four to five weeks, it was not free and it was far away from everything.

The basement apartment was perfect; it was roomy, had a nice yard for the puppies and such a quiet place. We prayed for favor with Craig, as we do our work here, maybe he would allow us to stay at least three weeks.

I woke up the following day, Wednesday, June 17*th* and discovered a problem. Our bodies were still on San Diego time. We accidentally stayed up late without even realizing it was past 1:00 am, Eastern Time. Not good for early morning "reveille". We had been trying to wake up at 5:00

am; I don't know if Beverly is sleeping on her alarm or shutting it off. Rhonda snores like a freight train all wrapped up in her grandma's blanket, and Jill is way underneath her blanket wrapped in puppy dogs. Kaweah took one of the private rooms, she is snoring like a caboose, and I have to admit, I'm sleeping like a baby, swinging in the lullaby tree.

When I woke up that morning I realized it was daylight already. I jumped out of bed to discover it was 8 am. Maybe Craig's house is too comfortable. I ran into the other rooms shouting, "Get up, get up, we are not on vacation," Of course, they all crawled out of bed with snail-like speed. For our first day of laboring in Atlanta we decided we would just regroup and have a team building meeting. It was one of those meetings, after being in tight quarters, just a little "iron sharpening iron" time. Once the air cleared and all the sparks fizzled out, we read our Bibles, prayed, and forgave each offense. We were ready for the presence of the Holy Spirit once again.

Now that we are in this little apartment we need a few amenities, like dish soap, toilet paper, and a little bit of food because we have a stove and refrigerator, yahoo! No more dollar meals for a while. This day will be for getting our bedding squared away, unpacking our tracts, and preparing for tomorrow, we will head to downtown Atlanta.

Thanks to everyone who prayed for Craig, when we arrived, I discovered he was just laid off from his job. Before we left, he had a new job. Even though he lost his job, he took us in and didn't charge us one penny.

Craig is an awesome violinist. When we said yes, we would love his basement home, I asked him to play a sample of his violin. As we were leaving from our first interview with him, he asked us to come on upstairs. He took us upstairs to his little entry room; there was a music stand, violin case and couch. He sat down and said, "I have been practicing this little piece." as he held up Bach, I had to laugh, "Ok, Bach?" I knew he was a genius. He turned around, pulled out the violin, reached for an old Baptist hymnal and he played about three short songs. Craig has an amazing gift playing that instrument. I'm excited to see everything the Lord has planned for this man; we found another one of God's hidden treasures in Craig Hill. We will continue to pray for the blessings of Abraham to be upon him.

We set the alarm for 5:00 am on Thursday, June 18th because we had to get our bodies and minds accustomed to Atlanta time, meaning it was actually 2:00 am, San Diego time. What a sight to behold. Have you ever watched the Bride of Frankenstein in the old black and white films? That morning, these five women walked around looked and acted like Frankenstein's brides, at least we were up. We were cleaned up and dressed first, and then Jill made breakfast. Guess what we had? Ramen noodles and eggs, Korean style, scrumptious, tasted better than a 99¢ hamburger.

We checked our bags to see how many gospel tracts we had left, my initial plan was to try and pack 500 tracts for each of us. I discovered there are over 5 million people in Atlanta and the surrounding area. I thought LA traffic was bad,

Atlanta was very similar. We had our gospel tracts in hand and decided to tackle the drive into downtown Atlanta. We thought we would take the MARTA train, the public transportation, but discovered the cost was $13 per person; it would be cheaper for us to drive.

We finally made it through traffic into downtown and found the park Craig told us about, Centennial Olympic Park. We had to park in a paid parking lot; we found one for $5 for the whole day.

When we stepped out of the car, "BAM," we were hit with severe heat and humidity. As we stood outside the car and looked at the park, thousands of people were everywhere. I thought to myself, "This is a great place for revival!" We headed across the street into the park and as we waited at the stoplight, there was also a strong stench, the typical smells of the inner city overrun by homeless vagabonds, living on the streets and temperatures only magnified the odors.

The devil knew we were there too. We were armed with tracts in hand and wasted no time, before crossing the street we started witnessing; we were completely surrounded by people. As we headed into the park, I noticed great big, plastic blow up movie screens. At night they were going to have a movie in the park, we were told there may be over 6,000 people there tonight. At midday, thousands of people were already there.

Beverly reached out to witness to a man and instantly he started to raise his voice and make a big scene. The unseen forces of darkness held his mind and body completely hostage. He was Muslim with a black bandana, he started screaming and hollering. At the same time, the team spread out and started witnessing to others. Rhonda carried her keyboard purse, ready to set up and play at a moments notice. Kaweah always brought her music just in case we could find an electrical plug to set up church. We took no more than ten steps and everyone began to witness, when suddenly, mega monster speakers came on out of nowhere and about blew out our eardrums. We found ourselves witnessing in high volume. We all looked at each other and I said, "Do you think the devil knows we are here? We are not stopping, let's go."

I went directly to people who were setting up sound for the movie, the ones blasting the speaker. I just knew if I found speakers and amps there had to be a microphone somewhere close by. The young man looked at me as I said, "Do you need me to help with your sound?" He looked at our t-shirts, "Mission America, Our Hope Jesus Christ" and he semi-smiled. I asked him, "Are you a Christian?" He smiled and said, "Yes." I said, "We have a vocalist right here, can she sample your speakers and microphone?" He almost gave in then said, "No, I better not." One thing we accomplished while I was speaking to him, (at the top of my lungs to compete with the sound), he shut off the loud music, now we can go witnessing again, without feeling we need a blow horn.

I was saddened by what I saw in that park that day. Everywhere I went, some people were on crystal meth, so many people tormented in their minds, women dressed like harlots, and the park workers in a fog. So many people said they were Christians. I realized why God sent us to Atlanta, there is a force of darkness in this place that has blinded the hearts of thousands maybe even millions. The Apostle Paul wrote in the book of James 1:22, "But be doers of the word, and not hearers only, deceiving yourselves." There is a strong spirit of religious deception which has blanketed this major city and I have great concern for the condition of the Christians in this area. I am frightened and fearful for their souls.

We passed out hundreds of tracts in just three hours that day. We didn't just pass out tracts, we gave a clear witness, by the time we left, we prayed with 16 people to receive Christ. We cannot tell you how many demon-possessed people acted out when we came around them, there were so many. Kaweah walked up to a young lady who suddenly manifested, started acting like a witch. She approached the two attractive black women who were sitting together on a blanket on the grass, one had beautiful hair to her knees. Before Kaweah could say anything to her, she stayed seated and yelled, "You cannot ask me anything!" Because of the Holy Spirit within her, Kaweah's presence alone, set off the unseen forces.

Funny, a few moments later Beverly walked up to the same girl and she smiled at her and said, "We are Christians." Maybe Beverly should pray more, just kidding. One broken person after another, a young man named Artemis needed prayer for healing, I could tell immediately that his body was reeking of hepatitis. Another man, living on a different park bench was also sick in his body; he probably had a sexual disease.

We found a covered pavilion with shade from the hot sun and a small captive audience. I told the musicians, "Come on Rhonda," she was a little nervous, after all playing in this environment is different than playing in the safety of a church building. I looked at Kaweah and she looked at me with the familiar look, questioning, "Mom, are we singing?" I nodded and answered, "Come on, let's sing." I didn't wait for Kaweah or Rhonda to start, I started with, "In the Name of Jesus," and they joined in. Before we knew it, people were coming from all different directions. Some were sitting down at the picnic tables; we had church right there in Centennial Park. We sang about 5 or 6 songs.

As I looked around, I thought, "I'm going to preach as well." I started preaching and gave an altar call. As I looked across, I saw a precious black man listening to the whole sermon, tears were rolling down his cheeks, another gentleman came closer, he turned and was mesmerized and listened. Men, women, and children were sitting there listening. I shared about the urgency of the hour, it was time right then to receive Christ and serve Him fully, the last days are definitely upon us. I held an altar call and before you knew it our team was praying with different people throughout the pavilion. We were having church on a Thursday afternoon, in the midst of the enemy's stronghold in Atlanta, Georgia. The Holy Spirit came and we had dominion.

We headed out of the park back to the parking lot, we were all looking forward to turning on the air conditioner and getting a drink of water. When we walked up, I looked at the tires and they were locked down by a towing company. Beverly did not read the instructions, when she paid for the parking, she was supposed to leave the ticket in the window for the parking attendant to confirm that we paid. Beverly sheepishly pulled the ticket out of her pocket, she thought it was in a safe place. She immediately called the towing company and now we had to wait there until they arrived. Of course, they are not in a big hurry and there was another woman near us in the same predicament. We witnessed to her until the driver arrived and then we were headed to Craig's house. It was a productive day of spying out the land, and preaching the gospel in the heart of downtown Atlanta.

The city of Atlanta and the surrounding area is a harvest field over ripe for revival, multitudes of broken people to win for Christ. I was deeply burdened to set up our tent and start the meetings as soon as possible. I cannot express how grateful I was for those who held us up in prayer, especially because we needed a good location for our tent revival immediately.

As we headed out of downtown, we were so tired, the heat and humidity really zapped our energy. Now we were lost, the GPS did not have a signal and we left the map at home. We drove along as far as we could from remembrance; we could tell by the sun we were at least heading in the direction towards home. However, we were completely lost and needed help. Thank God for His mercy and grace, we

121

finally found the way home, by that time we were not just tired, we were "Starvin' Marvin!" I went to the kitchen to start dinner, the girls went to walk the dogs and before you knew it; we were settled to rest.

Craig came to the door to bring us a map to the MARTA. I thought, "Craig is very thoughtful and very kind, a map was just what we were looking for." He had a bigger surprise, as he looked at me with his straight-face, very serious look, he reached out his hand hurriedly and handed me five tickets with five passes on each ticket for the MARTA. I looked at him thankfully, I knew how much the tickets cost, and he just kept on blessing us. I said, "Thank you so much." I thought to myself, "I could not get over how kind Craig was to us. Then he turned around suddenly and walked away. The night before, he brought a TV and DVD player to our door along with the wonderful, "Highway to Heaven," television series starring Michael Landon in case we wanted to watch movies in the evenings.

Craig also connected wireless internet available to the basement apartment so we could use our computers. I tell you, God brought us to the home of one of the Lord's generous treasures. Thank God for Craig, I ask everyone who reads this story, to please continue praying for him. For all of you single women reading this, as of this publication date he is not married, "smile."

We were done for the evening; then the power went out about 8:00 pm after all, it was thunder and lightning storm season in the south. We were sitting in the dark, as the sun had just gone down. Jill was looking out the window, she was excited and called us over, "Come and look at the fireflies," I had never seen them before. I was waiting for Tinkerbelle to show up, while Rhonda was looking for a mason jar and asked, "Do you want me to catch some?" Rhonda used to catch fireflies when she was a little girl, she grew up in Arkansas.

As we sat in the dark, we discovered it was a power surge. Again, Craig came to our rescue, he brought us candles. Tomorrow my goal was to find a lot for our tent. I appreciate every person who prayed and interceded for us, we were able to send our prayer requests back home and via our website. There are millions of hurting people in need of Jesus, this is why we came, this is the purpose of A Touch From Above, Mission America.

It was Friday, June 19th. Our time clocks and bodies were finally getting adjusted to the time change. We drove around trying to find a lot and were unsuccessful so far. Everywhere we stopped, we would hand out gospel tracts giving a clear witness, so we could redeem the time in every task. I was getting restless; I knew we had to get the tent set up because of the great need to bring the light of Christ into the darkness which is destroying this city.

On Saturday, June 20th, I woke up early, the Holy Spirit urged me to call the Foursquare churches in the area, we went online and found the contact information on their website, we also brought the Foursquare directory with us. Everyone dressed and we headed out to meet the Pastor; his name is Trey and his wife, Gretchen, they are a great couple. I knew immediately, they were soul conscious. We parked the car and headed to the church doors, they were setting up for an outside event, even in this Georgia heat they were reaching out to the neighborhood children with the love of Jesus.

Beverly went over to find Pastor Trey; she introduced herself to Pastor Gretchen. Pastor Gretchen was focused with the children's church, she saw our team of five women and thought we were volunteers to help with the outreach; she tried to put us to work. Pastor Trey walked up and upon introducing ourselves, she apologized and smiled. We would have willingly helped also, but our focus was to drive around until we found a tent location, a daunting task in a large area. We had already been in Atlanta for six days and time was ticking away, I knew we could not just sit around and wait, either the Lord would open up a lot or we would head on to the next city. I do love to see pastors who work so hard in ministry, they are an awesome pastoral team.

Pastor Trey shared that 175 children prayed and made decisions for Christ through their children's ministry. After I heard that powerful report, I knew we were in the right place, and then we went inside to look around their building. Their church, Refuge West Foursqsuare Church was located in a medium sized strip mall on a street with lots of traffic. Their building was the corner store front with a large grass area, perfect for our tent. Since they were so busy with their children's event, we scheduled a different time to meet with Pastor Trey. We would meet on Monday, June 22nd to discuss all the details, at a favorite meeting place in Atlanta, Chick-Fil-A. When we walked back to the car, I felt really good, more than likely Pastor Trey would say, "Yes."

We were all excited as we drove away. Now, we could breathe so we headed to find an inexpensive breakfast. I did not want to worry the girls, but we were running out of money, we really could not afford to go out to breakfast, but I wanted to celebrate at the same time. In Atlanta, we also noticed their was a Waffle House on every corner, we heard so much about them, I pulled into the parking lot, this one was located a few blocks away from the church in Marietta. I was glad when I saw the inexpensive prices and on Saturday morning the place was packed.

My daughter knows me well, by now she could read my faces and knew how I looked and acted when money was getting short. As a single mother with two children, we went through many lean times together. Kaweah sat next to me and quietly asked, "Mom are you sure we can afford to eat out?" I answered her with a smile on my face, as I have through her whole life, "Don't worry, God is good. Let's eat." All of the tables were filled, so we decided to sit on the bar stools at the counter. There were exactly five stools in a row and one stool at the end of the counter which was taken, an older man was enjoying his breakfast. He looked like a hard-working man; he was wearing a uniform; work pants like grey-blue "Dickies," and a matching work shirt.

We ordered our breakfast keeping it to $5 a person, we were splurging. In the middle of our breakfast, Kaweah nudged my arm and whispered, "Mom, the guy is paying for our breakfast." I looked toward the cash register, sure enough the gentleman sitting right next to us was paying for our meals, he was talking quietly to the cashier, she said, "Yes, sir." He told her, "Make sure they get a piece of their favorite pie too." The waitress walked behind the counter while he was leaving and told us that the man paid our bill and bought us pie. There goes the diet. The man walked out the door quickly; we did not get his name. We asked the girls and the cooks if they knew him, they answered that they saw him before, but did not know who he was either.

I looked at Kaweah as tears welled up in her eyes, and she said, "God is so good mom, this is where he wants us." She was so touched by the man's generosity and God's goodness. All the waitresses at the Waffle House were really touched, and we were able to share with them about Mission America and what God was doing. They were excited and said they would come to the tent meeting, they let us hang a big poster on their community bulletin board, and they were sweet young ladies.

Since it was still early on Saturday morning, we decided to catch the MARTA; I decided to head to a place called "Five Points" in the heart of Atlanta, not far from Centennial Olympic Park. We had thousands of tracts in our hands and backpacks. We were prayed up for our mission, we start our day with an hour of prayer first thing. We waited at the bus station, figured out which bus would take us to the train stop.

On our first leg of public transportation, we rode the bus to the MARTA train to downtown. I could not resist the captive audience sitting on the bus with us, I thought,

126

"Let's sing." We started to sing and had everyone's undivided attention. I sat there for a minute and realized the Holy Spirit was doing a powerful work. The nudging that comes from deep within by the Holy Spirit said, "Stand up, proclaim the name of Jesus and give your testimony." I jumped to my feet immediately. When I get that urge, if I think about it for too long, I will talk myself right out of being led by the Holy Spirit. I have learned to **_just do it_**. I stood to my feet and the words came out like a fountain from heaven, I felt God's presence.

When we boarded the MARTA train, we started to sing and I began to testify. A lady started to cry, she was Jamaican and she was sitting two seats down from where I stood. She was on her way to the airport because her brother just had a heart attack. Another lady sitting next to the Jamaican lady could feel the presence of the Lord as well; I could see the goose bumps on her arms. It was so quiet; you could hear a pin drop, the Holy Spirit was there drawing men, women and children to the cross of Christ, the Lord wanted to save souls.

Beverly was at the far end of the train and said she could hear the preaching loud and clear, and she could see and feel the conviction of the Holy Spirit by the expressions of the people and their behavior. The Lord's power flowed down the entire hallway of that train car. People began to pray and get saved with us as we made our way through the crowd to reach those whose hearts were touched. Half of the people on that train started to clap when I was finished preaching, I never experienced a response like that before anywhere. I have been preaching and singing on buses, trolleys, trains and any form of public transportation for over 30 years. The Holy Spirit made His presence known, Jesus was there to heal and to deliver.

We finally arrived at our destination, Five Points. All I could think or say was, "Whoa!" There was an unbelievable flood of people everywhere. It was like the United Nations; black, white, Asians, Indians, you name it and they were probably there. Without delay, we all went into action in the MARTA station; we could not help witnessing immediately. I knew we were in for a "ride" as I looked around, I could literally feel the presence of strong demonic forces. Have you ever gone into a sauna room filled with steam, where you can barely breathe as you enter? That is exactly how thick the air was filled with the presence of evil and darkness; we could see the demonstration in the words and actions of the people.

We were surrounded by a force of darkness which was suffocating the life out of young, old, rich, poor, every race and creed. This destructive force is no respecter of persons, the evil was lurking on every corner, I instantly began pleading the Blood of Jesus over us and we continued on. We did not even make it up the stairs out of the train substation, and Kaweah ran right into a demon-possessed individual.

I was talking to three black men, one 70 years old, another about 50, and the other 25, I gave each one of them a gospel tract and began to testify about my life, they said, "I am fine." I looked directly into their eyes, and I knew I was speaking to a demonic religious spirit. I asked, "Are you

128

serving Jesus 100%?" The 70 year old was reeking of alcohol, by now it was early afternoon. He had been drinking so much; he began to yell, using some of the foulest language. He became severely agitated without notice, was slurring his words and tried to intimidate me as he leaned forward into my face.

I turned away from the man and started talking to the young man. I asked him, "If you died right now, would you make it into heaven and are you serving God 100%?" He was the only one who was honest. He stood back, bowed his head and answered, "I know the truth, but I am not 100%." I looked at him and said, "I respect you for your honesty, but you are still going to hell. Why don't you make a difference today and make a decision to live for Christ with all your heart?" He got tears in his eyes as I reached over and put my hand on his shoulder and said, "Young man stop playing around, I will never cross your path again until we get to the other side. You will either be in heaven or hell." The conviction of the Holy Spirit was so strong over him he bowed his head and prayed right in front of the big crowd including his companions, I knew he was serious.

As we made our way out of the train station's underground basement, we walked up the long set of stairs and onto the street. The unseen spiritual forces were so evident, it was as if I had taken off my natural eyes and was looking through spiritual glasses. I walked up the stairs; a 6'4" man with dreadlocks was selling cult books about every Eastern religion you could imagine and essential oils. To the left of him, was another cult made up of about 10 young men dressed in all white. They were holding the Bible and had an easel with a large picture of Jesus and a sound system to broadcast their heresy and deception. They were capturing the hearts and minds of the young black men who passed by. They were twisting and taking scriptures completely out of context. I think our team was shocked by what they saw.

Within less an hour of walking and standing on the street which made up the city center of one of the largest cities in the United States and the in the Bible belt, we talked to hundreds of people, who said they were Christians. The only problem was their lifestyle was in direct opposition to their confession of Christ: they were gang bangers, prostitutes, crack sellers, drunks, demoniacs, homosexuals, and an unbelievable number of transvestites, all who were confessing Christians.

What are the churches producing in Atlanta? Since I have shared Jesus with thousands in this area, it is obvious; the churches are preaching another gospel:

> II Timothy 3:1-7, "But know this, that in the last days perilous times will come: For men will be lovers of themselves, lovers of money, boasters, proud, blasphemers, disobedient to parents, unthankful, unholy, unloving, unforgiving, slanderers, without self-control, brutal, despisers of good, traitors, headstrong, haughty, lovers of pleasure rather than lovers of God, having a form of godliness but denying its power. And from such people turn away! For of this sort are those who creep into households and make captives of gullible women loaded down with sins, led away by various lusts,

always learning and never able to come to the knowledge of the truth."

II Timothy 4:1-4, "I charge you therefore before God and the Lord Jesus Christ, who will judge the quick and the dead at His appearing and His kingdom, Preach the word! Be ready in season and out of season. Convince, rebuke, exhort, with all longsuffering and teaching. For the time will come when they will not endure sound doctrine, but according to their own desires, because they have itching ears, they will heap up for themselves teachers; and they will turn their ears away from the truth, and be turned aside to fables."

Five Points in Atlanta is the hub for the demonic spirit of deception that has been loosed in the city and surrounding suburbs. I do not lay the blame to sinners, instead the blame falls at the doorstep of the Christian churches. I understand how the Apostle Paul felt when he went into Athens:

Acts 17:16-17, "Now while Paul waited for them at Athens, his spirit was provoked within him when he saw that the city was given over to idols. There he reasoned in the synagogue with the Jews and with the Gentile worshipers, and in the marketplace daily with those who happened to be there."

The saddest thing, the thousands of people we encountered in those few hours, thought they were serving Jesus, yet they have embraced and follow another gospel. This demonic force has not just crippled Christianity in Atlanta; it has paralyzed the power of the true gospel of Christ. Jesus was crucified for the truth which will set the world free from sin, destruction and hell. The condition of American Christianity in 2012 has little by little deteriorated due to this false gospel which is spreading like wildfire across the United States of America. I am sure a remnant of Christians have not "bowed their knee to Baal," in this city, **Romans 11:4**. Yet, an alarming number of believers in Jesus have bowed down to the god of this world. The blatant perversion of women with women in plain view, as well as men with men, by the hundreds, we are truly on the final countdown to the coming of the Lord.

> **Matthew 24:36-42**, "But of that day and hour no one knows, not even the angels of heaven, but My Father only. But as the days of Noah were, so also will the coming of the Son of Man be. For as in the days before the flood, they were eating and drinking, marrying and giving in marriage, until the day that Noah entered the ark, and did not know until the flood came and took them all away, so also will the coming of the Son of Man be. Then two men will be in the field: one will be taken and the other left. Two women will be grinding at the mill: one will be taken and the other left. Watch therefore, for you do not know what hour your Lord is coming."

These are the words of Jesus Christ and today, they have never been timelier than right now. As time passes, they will echo louder and louder until Jesus comes, America needs a miracle!

132

My son, Samuel Stines helping with tent

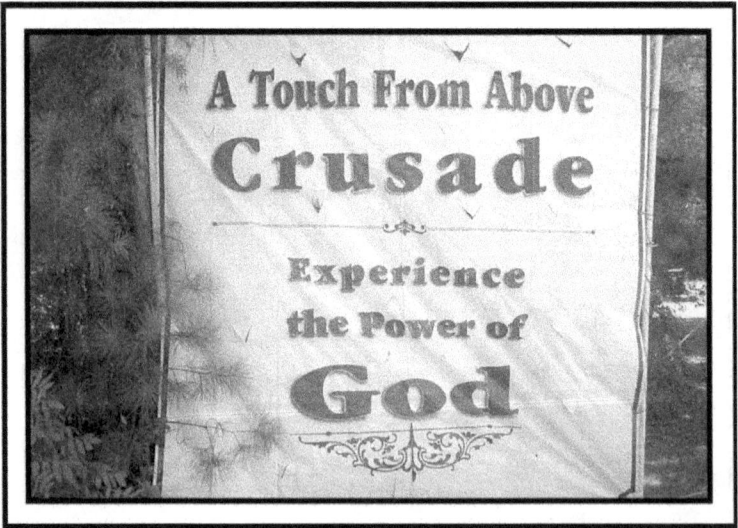

A Touch From Above
Crusade

Experience
the Power of
God

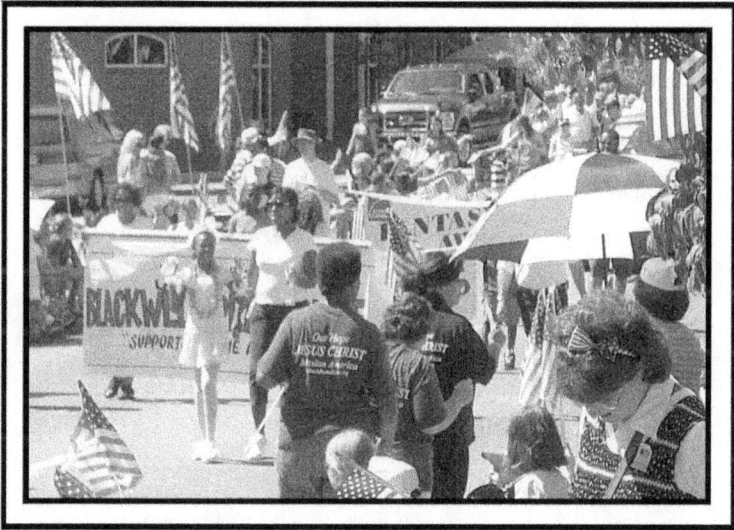

Chapter Twelve
Mission America Journey

How Can I Explain This?

I have been praying about how to write the report from our time in Atlanta, Georgia. I must admit it has been very sobering to my soul, piercing my soul in grief in a dimension I have never experienced in the last three decades as a Christian. I have traveled throughout the world. I ministered in areas submerged in the lowest depths of poverty. In the volatile bush of Africa; throughout Mexico, South Korea, Canada, and the Philippines via radio. Many places the Holy Spirit has sent me, I have seen with my own eyes literally thousands of hurting people receive Jesus in large meetings. I watched as many people walked to the meeting; traveling as many as four days barefoot, because they wanted their only pair to be in good condition for service. In other countries I found large groups of people who were hungry to hear the Word of the Lord.

From the time I purchased the revival tent in 2000, the Lord was moving me to take this trip; He put Mission America in my heart and I finally stepped out. The Holy Spirit kept trying to get my attention with the same nagging question "What about the United States?" Finally, I surrendered and said "Yes Lord, I will go, I will touch the US for you Jesus!"

As we took our tent down yesterday, Monday, July 6ʰ, I reflected upon the three weeks we spent in Atlanta. My heart will always be burdened and grieved for the people. Atlanta is a city rich in history, the beginning of many things here including a move of God long, long ago. There are large, pristine church buildings on every street, proclaiming the proud heritage of Baptists, Methodists, and Presbyterians. Not just a church on every corner, but massive church buildings everywhere you turn.

At the same time on major roads in the middle of every city in the surrounding area you will find cemeteries everywhere filled with the gravestones of souls long gone; the only remembrance of the mark they left upon the city.

The spiritual atmosphere is the same; church buildings by the thousands left as a remembrance of a long gone move of God. Buildings; and yet an eerie emptiness lurks there. The abundant life-changing gospel is missing in action. The fire of John and Charles Wesley, only a memory tucked away in books and carefully heralded in seminaries and libraries. The open air meetings of George
Whitefield only a memory, the history of the Methodists recorded in their founding documents and books. The religion which evolved has only left multitudes of people proud of their religious heritage with no sign of the repentance or right living which sparked the revivals of times gone by. Revivals led by men, who if they were alive to see what their denomination had become would be grieved and heartbroken beyond imagination.

What would they see as the current "fruit" of their denomination? Souls tormented by demons greet you at every turn downtown in the MARTA stations, Centennial Olympic Park and in Five Points. Some even quote scriptures and boldly proclaim they are "saved," yet they get angry after a few moments of hearing the true gospel of Jesus Christ.

Other "Christians" drunk, in gangs, bound in drugs, involved in homosexuality, some prostitutes, others preaching false doctrines on the streets. Many professing Christians compromising with sin while attending church, they are blinded, by the deception of demon forces that hold them captive, while Satan is waiting for their judgment to hell. There is more religion in Atlanta than I have ever seen before, which proves religion does not produce repentance, righteousness or revival. It is a very dangerous environment.

The cities are saturated with "church" and bankrupt of the gospel. The people are numb to their church programs; they just want to live in the world and still feel "religious." Many Pastors, ministers and preachers, including so-called, "Spirit-filled" churches are consumed in the new fad sent from hell "seeker friendly churches" while members grow in the thousands, they trade the pure gospel of Jesus Christ and the Bible for humanistic ideas, man's ideology, and fiction books. What happened to the Bible? Is the Bible alone not good enough anymore? Are man's ideas better than God's written Word which shall never pass away? This is another gospel! This is what the Apostle Paul warned us about. This heretical teaching is a trick from hell to steal the souls of men by the millions, its intensity and acceptance will only spread like wildfire as the day for Christ's return approaches.

I thank God for the small remnant of churches, pastors and Christians who are crying out for God in Atlanta, Marietta and the surrounding cities; they do need our prayers. Thank God for Minister Johnson, a seventy year old woman, an unsung hero of the gospel who is found every Saturday at her post on the corners of Five Points passing out gospel tracts and preaching the straight gospel with boldness in the midst of great darkness, her reward is great in heaven. Thank God for Pastors Trey and Gretchen of the Refuge West Church who have established God's love, power and

His presence in a storefront church in Marietta where the gospel is desperately needed.

Then there is the Korean church, Bethany Presbyterian Church in Marietta. The pastor gracefully welcomed me to minister and share about Mission America during their Sunday service on June 28th. This Korean church, out of the norm, for Presbyterian congregations in the United States, has Morning Prayer every morning at 5:30 am Monday–Sunday; we had the privilege of joining them on Monday, June 22nd for early Morning Prayer. This is an ordinary occurrence and priority, scheduled in Christian Korean churches across the world regardless of denomination. They share a building with other cultures and language congregations, the pastoral staff jokingly, made a statement which pierced my heart when we had coffee with them, they said, "If you want to speak to the English speaking Pastor come back for their 9 a.m. morning prayer meeting." I smiled, yet my heart was grieved for the truth to that statement, another reason I am building a Christian Prayer Mountain in Ramona, in San Diego County, California.

As we prepare to leave Atlanta to our next city, I saw with my own eyes what religion produces, spiritual destruction. My experience here only intensifies the burden I have for America. When the Holy Spirit spoke to me long before we left, I knew He brought us to Atlanta, Georgia to make impact in the streets, throughout the city, in marketplaces, parks, the Marietta 4th of July Parade, door-to-door in neighborhoods, and in every church service we ministered in.

We made impact for Jesus everywhere we went, including our six day tent meeting. This was the first time ever the tent was not filled. Those who did come to the tent were not church people; some very poor, broken, with no jobs. A slender, 50 year old black woman bound by alcohol came every night drunk. By the last night she was delivered and filled with the Holy Spirit. A precious young man who signed a major record contract, he toured performing R&B music. He walked into our tent meeting broke, torn apart by sin and hurt by religion. He repented, rededicated his life back to Jesus and was baptized in the Holy Spirit, speaking in tongues before our tent revival was finished.

We met a precious woman in the city park in Marietta one June 28th. After the service was over at the Korean church, Bethany Presbyterian, we headed over to the park and set-up an impromptu outreach service on the stage in the park. The woman was walking by with her husband and daughter; they stopped and stayed for the service. We talked afterward and a few nights later, she walked into our tent meeting. She confided in me, she had been a stripper for many years, she received Christ and repented of her sins.

My heart was deeply touched as I watched my son sit in every service of the tent meeting; I could see the Holy Spirit rekindle the fire of revival in his heart, a fire which burned in his heart long ago. He sat in services with his daughter, Anna and two sons, Zack and Josh. I know God sent me here to rescue them from the demon stronghold of religion which lurks right at their doorstep trying hard to take them captive.

There were many more people who came to the tent, and only on the other side in heaven will I see the greater impact of this tent meeting in Marietta, Georgia from June 30ᵗʰ – July 5ᵗʰ. As the last night's crowd was sparse, I said, "Lord, we've come all this way and even the offering was no more than $140 for six days." Within seconds the Holy Spirit dropped a word in my heart, "Did I not lead Philip into the desert to Gaza to touch one man in the chariot?" That was all I needed, I lifted my hands, wept and rejoiced in the same moment. I knew without a shadow of a doubt, the Holy Spirit drew those into the tent meeting whosoever would come. God's Word never returns void, **_Isaiah 55:11_**.

The last night we labored in the city, Tuesday, July 7ᵗʰ we went into a different area of downtown Atlanta. I was prompted by the Lord to go back one more time. I cannot stop saying how much of a blessing, Craig has been to us. He escorted us into areas that were bound and surrounded by darkness, sin, perversion, homosexuality, prostitution, drugs, transvestites; and it was thick like a fog.

As we continued walking around, lo and behold there was a giant building, a men's shelter with hundreds of men ripped apart by the destruction of sin. I went in through the massive open door; it must have been a former industrial building. I asked, "Who's in charge?" They sent me to a gentleman named Daniel, he was 6'4" tall and he looked down at me, as I looked up at him. I said, "Sir, please allow me to go in and speak to these men. Thirty years ago, I was broken and in a state of despair, bound up on drugs, then Jesus set me free." He looked at me, stopped and stared at me in silence for about a minute. I knew there was a war

144

raging between hell and heaven in his mind. I said, "Sir, they need the message I have about Jesus to find freedom. Please allow me to go in and minister." I pulled out my book, A Mother's Story and showed him the cover, I continued, "This was my life before Christ rescued me out of darkness," he was shocked at my pictures. He said, "Come back in 30 minutes."

We went out into the streets and ministered for 30 minutes, we were completely surrounded by the lost. Many received Jesus in a short time, reminding me of the scripture:

> **_Joel 3:14_**, "Multitudes, multitudes in the valley of decision! For the day of the Lord is near in the valley of decision."

Young girls as young as 15 ranging in age up to 60 years old prostituting their body's right before our eyes. The streets were streaming with grown men who proudly marched around flaunting their partial sex changes. Other men dressed as women, mocking us and quoting the scriptures; they were also prostituting in public and it was not even night time, it was daylight. We continued on and we saw the light of Christ break through the darkness in some lives before we made our way back to the shelter

We returned in 30 minutes as requested, I was allowed to minister to the giant room full of homeless men. Daniel even had a microphone set up. There were hundreds of people who had come to the end of themselves; homeless, food line, angry, no clothes, no money, and no baths. As each one took their seats, I introduced myself and brought Kaweah forward. I looked at her and said, "You are going to have to sing one of those powerful songs without any music; "In Heaven's Eyes," one from her CD, "He Is Risen."

She sang with anointing from heaven, like I've never heard her before. Everyone was captivated by the Holy Spirit which was coming from Kaweah's inner being. I saw grown men throughout the entire room weeping publicly, trying to hide their tears as Kaweah sang the sentence, "In heaven's eyes there are no losers," I knew this was God's appointment.

After she sang, I started to minister, preaching God's redemptive Word. I knew it was time for an altar call, their hearts had been moved and I had to give a bold call, I said, "Today you will make a decision, for those of you who would like to receive Christ, raise your hand now." As I looked around the giant warehouse of over 8,000 square feet covered with men; I saw hands raised throughout the entire place. I said to them, "You are going to have to be bold today, stand to your feet if you mean it, and come forward. I want to pray with you." To my surprise, they started coming one-by-one; almost 20 men came to the front for prayer.

I led them in a salvation prayer and I began to give them words of knowledge. These grown men started to weep, some sobbing. The Holy Spirit prompted my heart, "The gentleman on the side, the slender one is sick in his body." I leaned over and laid my hands on him, I prayed, bound up the spirit of infirmity and sickness, I said, "Leave him in the name of Jesus!" As we were leaving, a man walked up to me, with the same slender man, he asked me, "May I ask you a question, how did you know I was having an asthma attack? When you prayed for me, my lungs opened right up." The Holy Spirit moved. They will never forget that Jesus met them in that place; our last night in Atlanta was not in the newest church building with all the amenities, it was more fitting to end our time there in a homeless shelter, I think if Jesus was there in the flesh that is where he would have gone. To God be all the Glory.

What a powerful move of God; the Holy Spirit made impact, in three weeks we have seen over 120 people saved just in Atlanta, we lost exact count. In 47 days, since we left San Diego, the total amount of people who came to Jesus was 390 to that point. We handed out over 20,000 gospel tracts with a clear witness.

We took one day off, Wednesday, July 8th, caught up on our laundry, Kaweah and I spent the last day with my son Sam and family. We made the rounds and said our goodbyes to old and new friends. I planned on leaving early in the morning to make good time.

When I woke up that morning Thursday, July 9th, we were all so tired. We had been going and going for three weeks, once we stopped it was like we could not move any faster if we tried. We finally packed the vehicles and headed out on the road. We thought our destination would now be the East Coast to New England. The Holy Spirit has planned, Our Mission is America! Our Purpose is Souls!

147

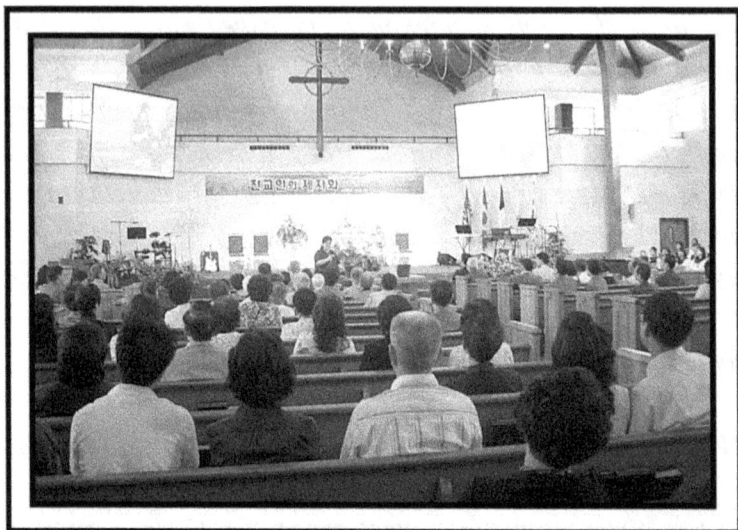

Chapter Thirteen
Mission America Journey

Burying the Past

*W*e drove out of Atlanta headed north on Thursday, July 9th; once again, we were not sure what to expect in the next city, we did not even know which city we would stop in. We started out later than normal; we were all moving kind of slow because we were tired. Once we were on the road, Beverly's cell rang, it was Craig. Although we had already said our goodbyes the night before, thanked him and prayed together, he wanted to make sure we were all right getting on the road. He asked what time we ended up leaving, the night before we told him we would leave first thing in the morning. Beverly answered, "Around 1 pm, we had to watch the last "Highway to Heaven," program. Craig laughed, he thought that was funny.

Within a few hours we drove into Columbia, South Carolina arriving in the early evening after stops for gas. We decided we would find a place to stay there before we continued on to the next city in the morning. It was still daylight so we headed towards downtown to check out the lay of the land.

I noticed a beautiful capitol building, right out of a movie. As I looked across the manicured lawn; I saw a small group of people and a man standing on the steps of the capitol building wearing a Ku Klux Klan outfit. I could not believe what I saw. I was not accustomed to seeing such symbols in California. The most interesting part was he was black, I am sure he was making a statement.

I found a place to park our truck and trailer, which can be a chore in downtown locations. We parked a few streets away from the capitol, we starting towards the people. As I was getting closer to the rally on the steps, I looked around at the statues and memorials encircling the park, there were wonderful sculptures, displaying South Carolina's history in the United States proudly, surrounded by beautiful trees and bushes. Then I looked up and another disturbing sight caught my eye, the Confederate flag was flying at the entrance to the park high above the city's center. When I asked around, someone said, "At least they removed the flag from the top of the capitol, that's where it used to fly."

After only being in Columbia for a very short time I could sense the strength of the spirit behind the Confederate flag; hatred and prejudice which is all rooted in pride. It is a symbol of a strong rebellion which was defeated in war, yet in the supernatural, 151 years later, the battle still rages. We were warned before we left San Diego to be careful about singing the, "Battle Hymn of the Republic," in the south. That is one of the songs on our CD, "Our Liberty," I thought that was ridiculous. Needless to say, Kaweah sang the song in Atlanta, we do not shrink back to the intimidation of the enemy.

It did not take a "rocket scientist," to discern the strongholds of South Carolina; they were clearly spelled out to me. The Confederate flag alone flying in a city torn apart by racism from the past and was an outward expression of a stubborn spirit which is still alive and well in South Carolina.

Columbia is a very beautiful city, with magnificent trees and beautiful, sweet smelling flowers blooming everywhere, at the same time symbols of darkness appeared in the same landscape, a visible and spiritual contrast. To see this man boldly parading around in a Ku Klux Klan outfit representing reverse hatred and pride, in 2009, this deeply entrenched stronghold captivates not only this city but the entire state and bleeds across the southern region of the United States.

I knew within minutes of arriving the Lord was revealing strongholds of this area and it was clear we were in the right place. The city and state are in need of a touch from Jesus, and its people who need more than just church, but healing deep within the core of man's heart. I could not just stand by and watch so I headed towards the platform on the capitol steps, where the organizer of the rally stood with a microphone.

I told the master of ceremonies I just arrived from San Diego, California via Atlanta, Georgia. I explained who we were and about Mission America, then I asked her if I could speak. She welcomed me with open arms because she thought we drove across the United States for the rally. The group advertised their event on Facebook.

As I stood there waiting for my introduction, I asked the young man standing next to me, "Why are these people assembled here?" He told me, they were there in protest of the moral failure of their conservative elected official, Governor Sanford. He was just caught in adultery and it was splashed all over the worldwide news. We were so busy in Atlanta and happily did not have television; I did not have a clue.

Another stronghold revealed in the Bible belt, a professing Christian politician secretly committing adultery for years on his faithful Christian wife and mother of his children. The outcome of religion without righteousness breeds secret

151

sin, lurking behind the scenes in the dark. Sins committed, not just by trusted political leaders, but confessing Christians.

> ___Joel 2:17___, "Let the priests, who minister to the Lord, weep between the porch and the altar; let them say, "Spare Your people, O Lord. And do not give Your heritage to reproach. That the nations should rule over them. Why should they say among the peoples, 'Where is their God?'"

As I stood waiting for my turn to speak, I asked the Holy Spirit under my breath, "What should I say?" Within less than two minutes my name was called. I thanked everyone for coming, then I cried out with boldness, calling for Christians and every American at every level to live according to God's standard, to live for Jesus Christ with all their hearts. I explained the cause of moral failures in our government is the result of turning our backs on the foundation of our country; the Bible, Jesus and Almighty God. I was amazed, caught by surprise at the unbelievable positive response as the audience roared and clapped.

How long has it been since somebody stood boldly for Christ on those capitol steps? How long has it been since God's Word was proclaimed in power on those capitol steps? As I finished speaking, I handed the microphone back to the host, the people continued to clap. When the rally was over I walked down the stairs and was further surprised by the media attention. I looked around and noticed; CNN, Fox News, the other local TV networks, newspaper and radio reporters. I was approached and interviewed by several from those media outlets. God was working out something for a bigger plan, while we were in Columbia and beyond, He would reveal the whole plan in His time. From the moment we took the exit off the Interstate in Columbia, South Carolina to the end of the rally, around 30 minutes had passed.

We never know where we are going to stay; a motel, campground or someone's home. We pray, "Lord, please open the door for affordable lodging." It was getting later and dusk was upon us, I knew we needed to find a motel immediately. Here we go again, stinky, stinky, and stinky; this motel was the worst so far. I'm learning to just hold my breath. I said, "Ok, this will only be for one night." I should have gotten the clue when I was in the lobby checking in and another woman was checking out. She was not discreet about how disgusted she was with her room she had just checked in moments before we did. What can I say, I was tired and the girls were tired too.

As they were walking the dogs, they noticed a massive contingent of two-inch long cockroaches, marching by the hundreds as if in military formation or a parade. The cockroaches were running around outside the motel, making a "b-line" from the trash dumpster outside to the motel sidewalks and running all over the parking lot. The girls didn't tell me until after we checked out the next day, thanks girls! I knew the Holy Spirit told me, "Keep your bags zipped tight," for a reason.

The next morning, Friday, July 10th, my spirit was deeply troubled after the sights, sounds and events of the day before; I will never forget the sight of the black man dressed in the KKK sheets and the other signs of supernatural forces of darkness. I asked the girls if they would give me some time alone, I needed to really pray and intercede. During my time of prayer, I was strongly urged by the Holy Spirit to contact the Foursquare Church in the city. Everyone came back after a few hours, it was time to check out, and we packed and were ready to leave. I had Beverly find the phone number and address for me. The idea kept going through my mind, "Contact the Foursquare Pastor."

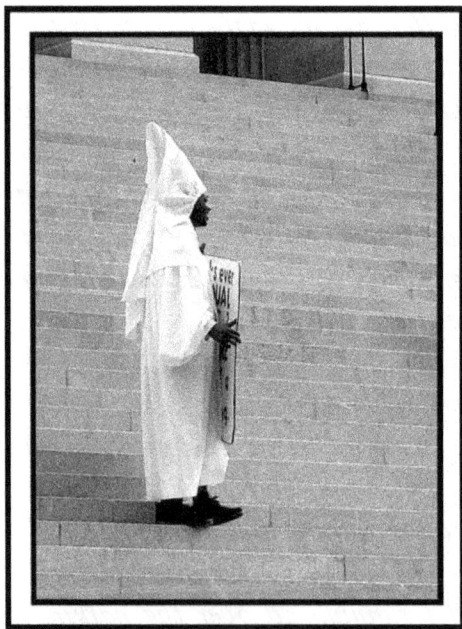

We loaded up the vehicles and entered the address for His Way Inn Foursquare Church in Columbia, Pastor Jack Deardorff. Off we went, heading towards the direction of the church. On the way, I noticed a campground, "Okay, campground or cockroaches? Which was worse, cockroaches or campground?" It was a no-brainer, campground here we come. We were willing to suffer through hot temperatures, humidity and mosquitoes; we were actually excited about the campground. Ok, so it was not like the wonderful Blessing Retreat Bed and Breakfast in Prescott, Arizona or Craig's nice basement apartment, at least we escaped the cockroaches and we had fresh air. It was a very nice campground too.

We kept driving and ended up in a housing development, I questioned Beverly, "Are you sure you have the correct address?" She said she was sure. I was puzzled, "Where is a church around here?" We continued on and ended up at the end of the road in a cul-de-sac. The address was clearly displayed on the curb, pointing to a beautiful brick house. I thought to myself, "Oops, Beverly did we make a mistake?" Even though logic told me, "This can't be right," for some reason, I did not want to turn around yet. I asked, "Beverly, knock on the door and see if this is the Pastor's house." A gentleman came to the door; his little Dachshund was barking up a storm, he had a phone in one hand because he was talking to a computer technician for his broken printer. Beverly stood on the porch while the man finished his phone conversation at the door at the same time he looked beyond her to see our great, big trailer sitting in front of his house. The trailer was our driving billboard, "Mission America, Our Hope Jesus Christ." The man smiled and now there was a visible twinkle in his eye, he motioned for all of us to come on inside.

The mystery began to unfold; the man was Pastor Jack Deardorff. He finished his phone conversation, while we were all sitting in his front room. He saw our t-shirts, "Mission America" and asked us to share our mission with him. I could tell by his expressions, he was a little stunned and surprised, but I could see by the Holy Spirit there was something stirring inside of him. All of the sudden, he said, "I was just praying this morning asking the Lord, 'What are we doing God?" He continued, "Then you guys show up at my door." He said, "Wow, what is God doing?" We talked with Pastor Jack for about an hour; we could tell we were one in Spirit. He asked us to come back for dinner, "Let's share a meal." His wife, Rebecca (Becky) was at work; we shook hands and left his place.

By this time, it was 2:30 pm, we headed somewhere for lunch. We drove around looking for an inexpensive place to eat; we found a restaurant close by. We were hot, tired and hungry; we knew we needed to eat and set up at the campground for the night. We could not leave the dogs in the car, we took shifts eating; one person would take a turn to sit with the puppies in the shade. While we were sitting down at the restaurant, a precious family came walking in, I noticed the wife as she kept trying to read the message on the back of our t-shirts, "Mission America, Our Hope Jesus Christ, atouchfromabove.org." I just smiled at her as she passed; I nodded my head and said, "Hello."

We finished our meal and as we were walking out, I turned the wrong way to get back to the truck. We had to walk all the way around the building to head in the right direction in the parking lot. We passed the outdoor patio of the restaurant where the same family was sitting. I was the last one to pass by, when the girls passed the family I noticed the husband and wife were both trying to read the t-shirts. I stopped and said, "We are five single Christian missionaries to America, traveling to every state to tell people about Jesus." I shared with them, "We left 47 days ago from San Diego and we prayed with over 390 people, and handed out over 20,000 gospel tracts." The husband was so touched; he jumped up and asked, "Can I please pray for you?" I was moved by his compassion and thoughtfulness to pray for us. We gathered around and he led us in a powerful prayer, asking God to protect us and keep us in the palm of His hand. I almost started to cry, I felt such compassion, the Holy Spirit was all over him. We said, "God bless and thank you."

We made it back to the truck and as I sat down and was about to shut the door, when a vehicle like a black SUV came around the corner. This same precious man who just prayed for us, reached out and gave me $100, he said, "Here just a little bit of something." That precious man did not know he just filled both of our gas tanks and paid for our campground for the night. I knew we were in the right place.

After setting up camp, we went back to the pastor's house to meet his wife, Becky. The Deardorff's are an incredible couple, both filled with the Spirit. We sat around their table, had dinner, and shared about God's goodness, mercy and grace. We shared how God always shows up just in time. They were so touched and we were too. Before we knew it, Pastor Jack brought communion to the table, while we sat around that table, the Holy Spirit showed up; all of us felt God's presence as we prayed, cried and thanked God for His grace which is always sufficient. By this time it was almost midnight as we stood up to leave, Kaweah sang a few songs and we gave our hugs to say goodbye. Becky said, "You girls can stay at our house, we welcome you in the peace of God." She said, "I have enough beds." We told her we had dogs, they just smiled and said, "See you tomorrow; there is plenty of room for everyone." They had two spare bedrooms and a family room above the garage, the three Deardorff children were grown and lived out of town. We thanked God on our way back to the campground; the time was 1:00 a.m. when we arrived. We just had church, on a Friday night, Book of Acts style.

We woke up on Saturday morning, July 11ᵗʰ at the campground. Beverly slept in the back seat of Rhonda's car and the rest of us split up in the tents with the puppies. We showered and packed up the camp, and gladly headed to the Deardorff house, they were a tremendous gift sent by God. We took time Saturday to set up our rooms at the house then we decided to head over to the mall near the neighborhood because we wanted to look for a lot for the tent.

We drove into a beautiful, outdoor mall surrounded by condominiums, a roundabout, and a large water fountain in the center. Lo and behold, guess what I saw? A covered pavilion used for music concerts with benches throughout and lots of people. Kaweah started singing and more people came over to see what was happening, then I lifted my voice and started preaching in the market square in the suburbs of Columbia, South Carolina. Once again, I was surprised by the positive response. We must have witnessed to over 50 *people and prayed with a few for salvation. The people were so open there, they were kind and honest. The Holy Spirit was already doing something special in that place.*

Since the next day was Sunday, the pastor invited us to his home church; Kaweah and Rhonda led worship and there was a powerful presence of the Holy Spirit. The people were so hungry to experience more of God in their lives. I shared a message about the Holy Spirit; how to be led by the Spirit and the importance of the baptism of the Holy Spirit. We prayed for those who wanted more of God. The pastors were so hungry for a deeper walk with the Lord as well. We had a great time. That evening, we went back to the mall with the pastors, this time we did one-on-one witnessing, over 10 people prayed for salvation; we talked and prayed for many others who are broken and searching for answers for their lives. This has been the Book of Acts experience in Columbia, South Carolina as well.

I was troubled because I could not find a place to set up our big yellow and white tent, yet God always has a bigger plan in the end. The Holy Spirit woke me up about 4:30 a.m. on Monday, July 13th. I lay in my bed, praying and asking the Holy Spirit, "What are we supposed to do?" I thought about the capitol building and lay there, asking the Holy Spirit, "Are you trying to tell me something?" All of the sudden, it hit my heart; "Mission America," the capital, "is the official seat of government in a state, seat of authority for every state, and government decision which impacts the whole state. I was seeking and waiting for clear direction from the Holy Spirit before I took the next step:

Romans 8:26-28, *"Likewise the Spirit also helps in our weaknesses. For we do not know what we should pray for as we ought, but the Spirit Himself makes intercession for us with groanings with cannot be uttered. Now He who searches the hearts knows what the mind of the Spirit is because He makes intercession for the saints according to the will of God. And we know that all things work together for good to those who love God, to those who are the called according to His purpose."*

Now, I had our marching orders direct from the Holy Spirit I was ready to share with the team. Jill, Beverly and I would go into the city to make a few appointments to start the "ball rolling". My experience has been to send out press releases to alert the local media outlets, part of my morning prayer requests were for wisdom in how to work with the media in Columbia; I saw firsthand the great turnout for the protest rally on the first day. All Glory to God, within an hour, we had set up a three day meeting on the capitol steps; another two day meeting at the mall close to the Deardorff's housing development.

Bingo! Then we met a wonderful gentleman from ABC, their office was directly across the street from the capitol. He knew everything about media and he was a Christian who helped us without hesitation. He walked us into the ABC building past security and took us into their Conference Room. He asked us what our mission was about. I told him, "I have been praying for God to help us find someone who could give us wisdom for media and marketing." He stood up, went to the other room and pulled

out a phone book, walked back and wrote out a plan for us.
This is another good example of the Lord confirming His
plan for us, everything fell into place without resistance in
answer to specific prayers. I knew we were in the right
place and the right state. The Holy Spirit is going to do
something very powerful in these meetings.

We appreciate every prayer from those who agreed with us
locally and across the miles and oceans. These cries of
agreement to the Lord probably ranged from whispers to
weeping to shouting, each started at individual points
across the United States; and culminated like nuclear fusion
in heaven then returned to our exact location with laser
precision to bring answers, wow God! The power of prayer
destroyed and bound up the lingering stench of rebellion,
pride and hatred.

We had a full schedule of ministry over the next few days; I
cannot reiterate how we could not have accomplished these
tasks without a powerful contingent of prayer warriors,
thank you all. No one and I mean no one can prove that
God does not answer prayer. During my 33 years as a
Christian, I have enough proof of answered prayer to silence
any critic.

Psalm 145:18-21, "The Lord is near to all who call upon
Him in truth. He will fulfill the desire of those who fear
Him; He also will hear their cry and save them. The
Lord preserves all who love Him, but all the wicked He
will destroy. My mouth shall speak the praise of the
Lord, and all flesh shall bless His holy name forever and
ever."

I ministered in the open air at the South Carolina capitol building in the very same spot where the man with the Ku Klux Klan sheets was standing. The difference was I stood there in the name of the Living God of Israel, Jesus Christ, my Lord and Savior.

As young David stood against Goliath, the Philistine giant who ridiculed the armies of Israel and boldly mocked God Almighty. David had confidence in the Lord and he answered the call which seasoned warriors shunned; he went without weapons of war. He stood there with stones and defeated the enemy on the field that day:

> *I Samuel 17:50-51*, "So David prevailed over the Philistines with a sling and a stone, and struck the Philistines and killed him. But there was no sword in the hand of David. Therefore David ran and stood over the Philistine, took his sword and drew it out of its sheath and killed him, and cut off his head with it. And when the Philistines saw that their champion was dead, they fled."

I stood on the steps of that building to tear down this giant stronghold in South Carolina; he must bow and be defeated in the name of Jesus, as Goliath was destroyed on the field of battle. From the days of war in the Old Testament when the soldiers fought with swords, Jesus transformed the methods of warfare to spiritual armor and weapons fashioned for a battle in the heavens, the most crucial piece of armor, "praying always with all prayer and supplication in the Spirit,..."

2 Corinthians 10:4, *"For the weapons of our warfare are not carnal but mighty in God for pulling down strongholds, casting down arguments and every high thing that exalts itself against the knowledge of God, bringing every thought into captivity to the obedience of Christ, and being ready to punish all disobedience when your obedience is fulfilled.*

In Columbia we were welcomed by Pastor Jack, and his remarkable wife, which I must call Pastor Rebecca, they pastor a Home Church. They are faithfully laboring to see the Kingdom of God expanded, not only did they open their home for us, they labored together with us at each of our meetings to see souls saved.

They were excited to receive the new believers into their Home Church, the young men who the Lord touched in a special way during the meetings at the on the capitol steps. Eddie is a gifted man, a commercial plumber. He found himself caught in the downward spiral of the economy without a job; he lost his family, and ended up homeless. He was in one of the hardest trials of his life. I met him one night after we ended the service at the capitol. Eddie heard the music and preaching because he was walking through with a rolling suitcase, looking for a place to sleep. He hadn't taken a shower in a few days, who knows how long it had been since he had a shave and haircut. The Holy Spirit drew him to the cross that night and the Lord touched Eddie in a special way, and renewed his hope.

Another young man, Robert was 27 years old at the time. His mother was a crack addict and Robert was thrown into the "system" at 10 years old. He was a broken little boy who the devil was trying to destroy through rejection. From a young age, he learned how to survive on the streets. I was truly amazed to see how the Holy Spirit drew him to the meeting; the Lord saved him, and filled him with the Baptism of the Holy Spirit, speaking in tongues. Robert stood on the steps during the altar call and publicly repented, and spoke in tongues in front of everyone. Filled with the joy of the Lord, Robert shall never be the same. Now locked in the home church; he is getting ready to be baptized in water. I believe he will one day preach the Gospel of Jesus Christ.

Jayson who just graduated from the University of South Carolina, passed by one of our Mission America fliers, and was drawn to the meeting, called to be a prayer missionary, a gift to the body of Christ. I shared with him how important it is to pray in the Spirit, he listened and was open to learn.

In conclusion of our first tour of Mission America, my heart was touched so deeply words cannot express. Arriving home, thinking over all the Lord had done in just 62 days. Looking around in my front room at all the things I have collected throughout the world while out ministering, things from Africa, Korea, Canada, Israel, England, on and on, yet it is amazing how much stuff one really has. As I went from room to room I thought to myself, what is all this in light of eternity?

Mission America, first journey 6,000 miles, so many people were touched by the grace of God, I wonder how many more were touched and said nothing. How many people driving in their car thinking life is too hard, when all of a sudden this truck drives beside them, "Mission America - Our Hope – Jesus Christ!" When I stand on the other side only then will we really see all the Holy Spirit did.

As I sat in my comfortable chair singing aloud in the solitude of my own home after 62 days of having people around me 24/7. I sang, "Lord Make Me an Instrument," I began to weep and rejoice 444 people saved, 75 people filled with the Holy Spirit, one church started, 20,000 gospel tracts given out; tears of joy! I also think about all the wonderful people we met, Pastor Jay a humble man and his amazing, gifted wife Linda; they opened their home "Blessing Retreat" in Prescott, Arizona and their hearts to receive us in the Lord.

The young couple in Texas, who are pioneering their first church, Pastors Jon & Ashley, who when no motel or campground was available they opened their church doors, for us to rest and sleep for the night.

The amazing man gifted with a camera, yet color blind, this tall gentle, unique 6'5" man named Larry, hidden away in a little trailer park with his Bible, and in love with Jesus, he will have a wonderful book out soon.

Pastor Trey, and his beautiful wife Pastor Gretchen, who labor in an area filled with religion in Marietta, Georgia, yet a light shines brightly, in the corner of a little market mall, as hundreds of children come to Jesus, this couple prays as they are praying to win the parents into the Kingdom of God.

Craig a remarkable young man in Atlanta, Georgia, who has many talents, from violinist to computer skills, the list goes on; he opened his home to accommodate five missionary women while we labored in the streets of Atlanta, GA. I know the Lord has a special woman who will be this man's wife. Also his brother who came to visit Craig, while we were there, offered to open his home when we go to Florida.

Hundreds more people were saved, and many more people touched my life, it would take a journal to write them all in, and maybe one day I will. What is one soul worth? The Wonderful Cross! One person is so valuable to the Master, thank you Jesus for the hundreds of people who made a decision for Christ on the first leg of our trip!

While this comfort in my home is wonderful, and the quiet time is priceless, yet I am excited to step out once again on the road across the whole USA to reach more people for Jesus. I am saved to save! Jesus paid everything he had for one soul! That painful Cross, yet so precious and dear when one lost soul comes beneath the flood; the blood cleanses white as snow.

A highlight of this first Mission America journey was meeting so many wonderful people, people who shined with the true love of Jesus. They were kind, and filled with excitement to collect the souls who were saved, ready to *labor, to help each new soul continue their growth in the grace of our Lord and Savior Jesus Christ.*

I am looking forward to see all the Lord will do on our second Mission America Journey! As we head out on the road to every Capitol, and state in America, proclaiming, this government will be on His shoulders! Jesus is Lord, calling our nation, America to remember our God, repent and cry out for our country.

Souls for the Kingdom, I must reach the lost, souls for the Kingdom won at any cost.

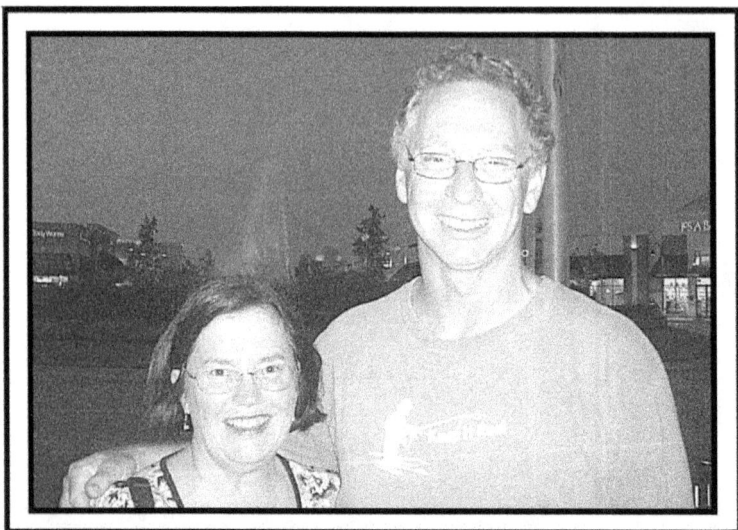

Pastor Jack & Becky Deardorff

Dr. Luauna leaning on statue of George Washington

"It is impossible to govern the world without God and Bible." George Washington

Chapter Fourteen
Mission America Journey

Tour Two Begins

*M*ission America Tour Two was non-stop, we were on the road for eight days before we could write; we covered five states and four Capitol cities.

Our good friends, Mark & Suzanne Olsiewski, offered to lend us their Chevy Avalanche truck with a king cab so we could get on the road before winter. With time in mind, we accepted their generous offer.

In the meantime we left Ramona, August 23rd early Sunday morning. Our first stop was Burbank, California; Pastor Hector's church gave us a warm welcome. We know we are with family every time we visit this church; they too hunger to see people come to Jesus. I shared with them about our daily radio program in the Philippines, the people rejoiced, the pastor wept with joy knowing we were reaching his native people. The Apostle Paul talked about churches which supported his missionary journey; this church is always so faithful to support us. As we placed our Mission America t-shirts on a back table after sharing about our travels across the U.S., Pastor Hector encouraged everyone to buy one. Through their generous giving they supported five nights lodging and three tanks of gas, and let's not forget the souls saved. This church will reap a great reward, I am grateful for Sun Valley Foursquare Church, great is their reward.

After the Sunday meeting we continued on driving as far as Coalinga, sharing the gospel with people at every stop. After a nights rest, the following morning we drove into Sacramento, for our meeting at the Capitol.

As I drove around the Capitol I could not believe the expressions of hate and disgust on the faces of some people as they saw our trailer. Setting up our flag and speakers on the Capitol steps, Kaweah began our rally with singing. I looked around and noticed people from different parts of the world at the Capitol; people from Spain, Ukraine, Mexico, China, and India, and of course Americans, about 125-150 people throughout the area. We could not help but notice some of the liberal Californians, as I stood up to speak, you could see some of the people manifest, screaming obscenities and giving me the "thumbs down." A young man came to sit down, enjoying Kaweah's singing, but between songs; he went to the table and proudly declared, "I am an atheist." Then he went back to sit down. Another woman over a half a block away was screaming and hollering filled with the devil trying to disrupt the whole service. I knew we were right where Jesus wanted us to be.

In spite of the craziness, that night five people received Jesus in Sacramento, on the Capitol steps. As we were packing up, a good friend of mine named Sofia, came up and stood as I was sharing Jesus with two women from Spain; I was trying to speak to them in Spanish. As I struggled with the right words, Sofia jumped in and interpreted, funny I thought this lady, was another one of their friends from Spain. Then I realized it was my friend, Sofia, I had not seen her in 27 years; we were both saved on the same day over 30 years ago. My eyes must have gotten big as saucers, as I realized who she was as she stood in front of me; there were hugs and tears of joy.

We had many years to catch up on in a short amount of time. She had been diagnosed with leukemia on her 50th birthday. Sofia had made arrangements with a friend for us to stay at their home. After packing all the equipment, we drove to Sofia's friend's home Heidi, Mike and their two children. They prepared two rooms for us. What an incredible couple, we had a kindred spirit, the Holy Spirit, in us makes us like family. Arrangements were made, Sofia would come to the house and we would have breakfast together. The Lord had a bigger plan!

The following day, Kaweah sang, and we were rejoicing in the Lord, we had a little home church service as the Holy Spirit's power came to visit. We prayed for Sofia; we bound up the spirit of leukemia, and I prayed for Heidi and Julie. God's presence was so strong, we were all in tears. I was so pleased to hear Sofia was not allowing radiation or chemotherapy; she had just started a new natural remedy. I was overjoyed, I know prayer, faith, and God's natural way is the best way.

After we said our goodbyes, my time with Sofia was just not enough, but we had to get on the road. We headed towards our next city; Salem, Oregon. Driving all day, we stopped in Medford, Oregon for the night.

Sacramento, California Capital

My friend, Sofia

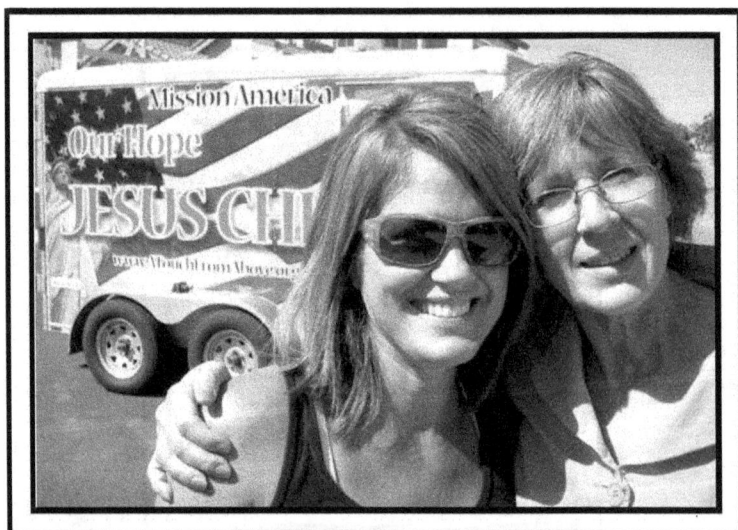

Heidi, our host & Sofia

Chapter Fifteen
Mission America Journey

God's Majestic Northwest

*W*e rested overnight and headed out in the morning to Salem, found lodging, unloaded the missionary dogs and prepared for the meeting at the Capitol steps that evening. Downtown Salem is so beautiful yet as you talk to the people or look closely into their eyes, there seemed to be numbness to the things of God. Inscribed on the building were themes of righteousness and morality in the center of the city and yet those passing by did not realize the importance of those quotes written so long ago.

The young people seemed so lost; many between 15 – 18 years old, boldly refusing Jesus Christ, some angry as they saw the message on the trailer, and heard the songs about Jesus. As we were already closing down I noticed a man in a wheelchair, with his caretaker who came to join the rally. I motioned for Kaweah to sing a few songs, and then I noticed tears were openly flowing down his cheeks while Kaweah sang each song. I knew the Lord had a plan for this man.

I gently laid my hands on his shoulder and led him in a prayer, and then I prayed for his healing. He was from the Ukraine, he became sick several years ago, a blood clot in his brain, before that he was a hard working man. This big, 6'4" tall man was now in a wheelchair, his wife left him and took his seven children when he became sick. I also prayed for the healing of his broken heart. He wept and after receiving a touch from the Lord he was a different man before he left that night.

Another dear friend, David who lives in Eugene drove up to the rally, it was so nice to see him. He was saved in my first pioneer church and we had a good time catching up. I will never forget this special man, David forever etched in my memory the day he was filled with the Holy Spirit, falling under the power, he lay on a cement floor, tears running down his face, while praying so gently in his prayer language. He will always be special to my heart; David is a true friend indeed. That night in Salem, Oregon, at the Capitol, we prayed with five people to get saved.

The next day, it was an early wake up and we headed to Olympia, Washington for our next stop, we had arranged for a meeting at 12:00 noon. Once again, there were people from different places, yet it was a bit quiet as we prayed for the state of Washington. Kaweah sang inside the Capitol center main hall, capturing the hearts of those who were in the range of her voice. We stepped outside as we were told we could not hold anything religious at the Capitol. Every place is different, but we established God's dominion in spite of it all. We shared with the people outside and stood boldly for Jesus. Five people were saved, to God be all the glory!

We immediately were back on the road because our next meeting was scheduled in Helena, Montana on Sunday. On the way there, we drove through some of God's most beautiful country, Washington, Idaho and Montana. We were trying to make it all the way to Helena, but it was getting late into the day, and I was getting tired of driving. I had Beverly call around for campgrounds, I prayed, "Lord, lead us," as I looked at the gas gauge, I was going to try to make it to the next larger town. All of the sudden, I felt the need to take the next exit. As we were filling up with gas, Jill was inside witnessing to the cashiers and Kaweah was outside talking to the other gas customers. An older gentleman drove up to Kaweah and asked her, "What are you doing?" As he looked at our trailer, Kaweah proceeded to witness to him, asking him if he was completely ready for Jesus. He answered, with confidence, that he was a Christian; and was a deacon at his church.

I rolled down the window of the truck and told him we were headed to Helena and asked if he knew of a safe campground. He asked what we sleep in and I told him we had tents, he said, he owned 400 acres and we could set up our tents on his property. I normally do not just follow someone to their place, but I knew this man was sent from God, we followed him to his property. He had two extra bedrooms and said, "You can just stay there and use the bathroom and showers in the house."

He was so kind; he showed us in and let us set up our dogs in the extra room. He said there were bears and wolves in the area. Yikes, we were glad we didn't sleep in tents. He even caught some grasshoppers and said we could go fishing. Driving day after day, fishing sounded like just the thing to unwind. After we unloaded, Jill, Beverly and I headed out with our fishing poles, (I packed them just in case we got real hungry…Smile!) Within minutes, on my first throw I caught a 27 inch trout and Beverly caught her first fish, dinner here we come. At dark we headed back to the house, I cleaned and cooked the fish. We were all happy to enjoy our freshly caught meal.

I shared with Mr. Tony about my testimony and Mission America. Every time I talked about a life being changed by the power of Jesus, his eyes would tear up; he was so touched by souls coming out of darkness. I knew he loved Jesus, and the Lord arranged for us to meet him. The next day, we went to church with Mr. Tony; he wanted us to share Mission America with his pastor and church. The pastors were kind and opened their door for us to share during their service.

I shared my story, the church was filled with visitors and the people's hearts were touched as I shared about the power of God which changed my life. As I looked across the church, I could see the Holy Spirit moving upon the hearts of the people, and in the back row sat Mr. Tony, when I reached the part of my testimony when someone witnessed to me; once again his eyes welled up with tears. Imagine this big 6' 3" hard working logger and heavy equipment operator, a good, old country boy in his late 60's, his heart gripped by the Holy Spirit, started to weep. He was truly a mighty man of God, gentle, yet powerful. He shared how he ran for the U.S. Senate; he is a warrior for God. I will always respect, and hold high regards for this man, who loves with the love of Jesus. May God grant him the desires of his heart, and bless his family, and his wonderful grandchildren.

Kaweah stood to sing; the people were encouraged and inspired by the touch from the Master's Hand. The Holy Spirit moved in this little church in the mountains of Montana. They allowed the team to set up a table for my book, put out our Mission America t-shirts, and music to help fund us along our Mission America Tour.

Later that day, we reached Helena, the Capitol of Montana, there were people again throughout the grounds. We again started with music, Kaweah sang, while the people were listening. I noticed a man boldly running right in front of us, up and down the steps. I started to share Jesus with him; he was about 75 years old. He stopped, looked me right in the eye, and announced, "I am Jewish!" "Perfect," I said, "so was Jesus," he said, "I don't need Jesus." I asked him, "Will you be like the children of Israel and reject Jesus?" I stunned him, he was bold enough to make remarks against Jesus, and I figured he came up to me first. He turned and walked away.

At the same time three teenagers walked up to me, and asked me, "What is Mission America?" I shared with them, the plan of salvation, and asked them to pray. They humbly bowed their heads, while the other Jewish man ran by; he was surprised to see these three wonderful teens pray. As I finished praying with them, one of the teens, had tears in his eyes, he said, "I always wanted to know why Jesus was going to judge this world. Now I know why, Jesus is the answer for the whole world." They were so open to learn, what a breath of fresh air they were, they made my day.

One shared how his mother was on drugs, and a mess, I gave him one of my books, and asked him to read it, and then give it to his mother. We prayed for their mothers, they were all from rough families. I know, "For such a time as this says the Lord...," Jesus died for these three young people and placed us in their path. God has a plan for their lives. We shared with about 75 people that day, including these ones who Jesus had an appointment with; three teens, they are the heartbeat of Christ. The military couple Jill prayed with and another young lady who prayed to receive Jesus!

As we left Helena, we ran into some strong rain, and a wind storm, I drove slowly and prayed in the Spirit. Thank God, we made it to the next campground. We came to a crossroad on the highway, I felt strong to change directions, and we would head towards Colorado instead of farther east. Later on, we would realize the importance of this decision.

Salem, Oregon Capital

Olympia, Washington Capital

Olympia, Washington Capital

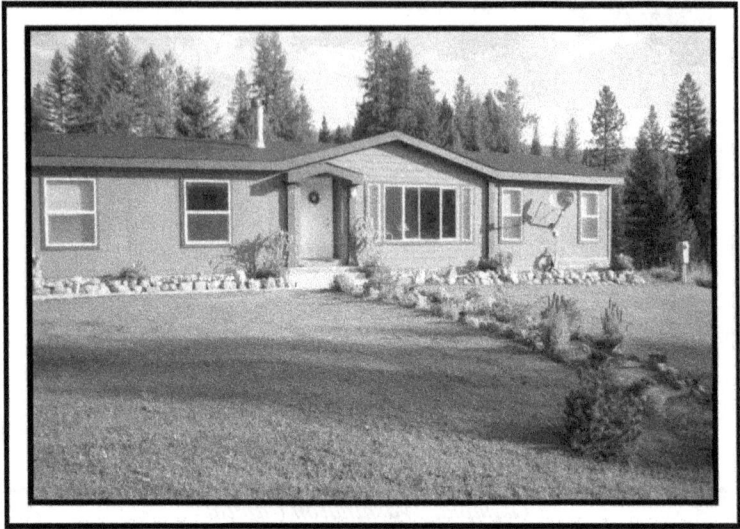

Mr. Tony's house & 400 acres

Helena, Montana Capital

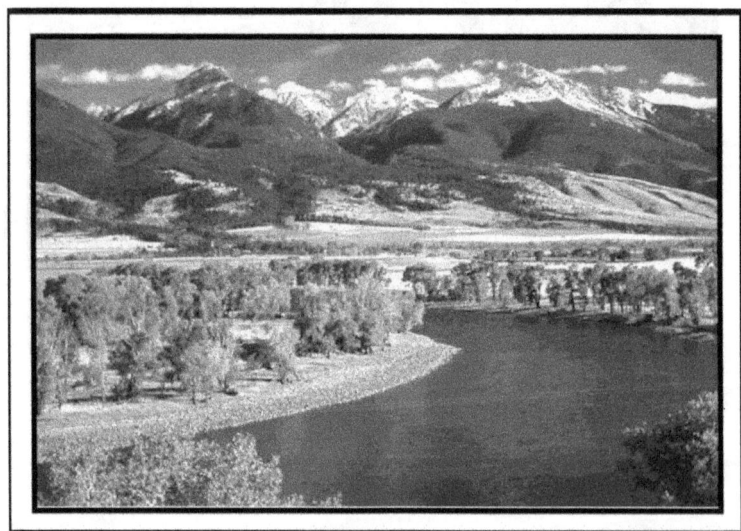

Chapter Sixteen
Mission America Journey

Pit Stop in Billings

*T*ime for writing and uploading was difficult on our second mission trip, finding a place to use the internet to upload has been even harder. At times we went through mountain passes and were unable to even have a phone connection.

As we drove into Billings on September 1st, I felt a strong urge by the Holy Spirit, to stop and find a KOA, and just to be still. I looked on the map for a KOA and bingo, we found one. We checked in and settled down for the night, not knowing why the Holy Spirit had us come to Billings; after all it was not on our schedule.

God's Word is so powerful, "Many are the plans of a man, but it is the Lord who puts it all together," I felt a strong urge to call a Foursquare church in Billings. Beverly made the call and at first it seemed non-productive, so I figured the following day we were going to head out. The next day Kaweah started packing everything, and again I felt uneasy as the Holy Spirit spoke to my heart not to leave Billings, Montana yet. I asked Beverly to check and see if it was ok to stay in our cabin another night at the KOA. I must say this KOA was beautiful but filled with mosquitoes, and we had no repellent, ouch!

Sitting in the cabin, praying, and thinking to myself, "Holy Spirit why are we here?" To my surprise, my phone rang, it was the Foursquare church secretary, Theresa. I told her about Mission America and what the Lord put on our hearts, we desired only to be a blessing to the church. I made sure she knew we are true missionaries to America. She said, "I saw your website, are you sure you didn't mean to call the big church?" The minute she said that, I felt the Holy Spirit speak right to my heart, "You called the right church." I told her, "You are the right church." I told her we were not asking for money, she said, "Why don't you come by the church and let's talk and pray." The team loaded the car and we headed to their church, only to discover, it was less than a half a mile from our KOA and it was in an area perfect for revival.

Going in to meet the secretary, Theresa, our team sat around the table, after about 30 minutes, Pastor Grove came in and sat down. As we shared our heart and mission, I could tell a thousand thoughts were going through Pastor Grove's head. He sat calmly and listened as we shared about our first Mission America trip, I could tell he was a bit nervous or unsure. I could see Pastor Grove was meticulous, just by meeting him, I could see he was a man who paid attention to detail, in his own words, he likes all of his ducks in a row. He must have stood up about four different times, getting a cup of coffee, answering a phone call. I reiterated, "We did not come for money, I know my calling is to preach the gospel."

The Lord put Mission America on my heart, we came to be a blessing, to win souls, and build up the local body. I shared, "We have our own fliers, we are His laborers, and we will work to blanket your city, to bring in the lost, if you allow us to have a three day meeting, we will see a harvest come in for Jesus." We talked for about an hour, as Pastor Grove's piercing green eyes looked at each of us intently, trying to figure us out, who is this group? I must admit, I noticed it was hard for some pastors to understand, why we were doing Mission America for Jesus. No strings attached, just to win souls for Christ.

Mission America was launched because so many people are lost and unsaved in America, I knew this firsthand since I pioneered my second church. Along with my experience as part of the largest Spirit filled church in the world, Dr. Cho's church, I know America is in great need for revival and a touch from the Holy Spirit.

Theresa said, "Let's go upstairs and pray," we went upstairs to the prayer room, we love prayer and I knew God wanted us in Billings. I knew even more so, because this was a praying church. We started praying in the Spirit, worshipping and praising God, after about 20 minutes, God's overwhelming presence was in the room I knew the Holy Spirit was doing something. I asked Kaweah if she had a song, she lifted up her voice and sang, "Amazing Grace." We continued to pray and Beverly began to prophesy about the Holy Spirit leading Cornelius to Paul in the book of Acts. Then we began to worship again, then we stood up and everyone said goodbye. No decision was made about the meetings when we left, but I knew Theresa was a prayer warrior. She said, "Just give Pastor Grove time to think about it, he is a good man, and he prays." Saying our goodbyes; Jill said, "We only want to be a blessing, please let us know as soon as possible, because if it is not God we will go to the next town."

We got into the truck with our Jesus trailer, we drove throughout Billings and caught the eyes of many people as we drove around the city. I saw so many broken people, casinos on every other block, and thousands of Indians and others in need of Jesus. I thought, "This place needs a touch *from the Master's Hand." When we returned to the KOA, I sat down on the porch swing, I felt like crying over Billings, Montana. "I prayed Lord we want to be a blessing, open the door You desire us to go through." Our team prayed again; "Lord, we want nothing but Your will." We knew Labor Day was just around the corner, we had to make some crucial decisions either to stay or go.*

Later that evening, my phone rang; it was Pastor Grove, he asked, "How can we work this out?" He said, "I don't think it would be good to do the revival this week, because many of the leaders of the church are on vacation for Labor Day." A decision was made we would attend the church on Sunday morning, Kaweah would sing, and I would share about Mission America, and our three day revival would start the following week.

We would trust God for lodging for the next ten days. When God opens the door, He always opens lodging. I knew He was going to do something great. After I hung up the phone, I shared with the team, "Hallelujah, revival in Billings!" We were rejoicing and praising God when the phone rang again, Theresa called, she had a place for us to stay, lodging was provided we would have a full basement, with bathroom, and our missionary puppies were welcome. I thanked Theresa, and said, "Ok, we have to plan; we must get out as many fliers as we can." A great opportunity, our team would have seven days to blanket the city with fliers. We were like horses biting at the bit, ready to labor for Jesus.

The following day we packed up our stuff at the KOA, and later met with Theresa. We pulled out our fliers; we asked for a map of Billings and prepared a strategic plan. I was excited to find a church ready to labor right beside us, to win their city for Jesus. Theresa was just as excited as we were, the moment I met her I knew she was an amazing woman, she had been praying about an outreach for the city. I shared with her that we would blanket the city 5-6 hours a day, Theresa was in tears, and she also went right to work preparing labels for the bottom of our fliers. To our surprise, they also prepared fliers; they had them printed on the back of our Mission America flier.

Later that afternoon, we went to meet the couple who opened their home to us, Chip and Diane, what an incredible couple. "Our house is your house!" We each set up our rooms, unpacked and got ready for our 10 day stay; we would be ready to labor.

The following day, our team was up early, 5:00 a.m., to pray for a few hours before putting out fliers. We headed out for the first day, we later discovered there was going to be a classic car parade at 7:00 pm. My heart skipped a beat, what could be more of a classic than our "Ancient of Days?" Jesus, He is timeless. We found out how to join the parade, our team went into action. What a great opportunity, I thought, "I mean if we are going to make impact, let's make big impact for Jesus."

Beverly signed us up for the parade and we were in the line of cars with our Mission America T-shirts on. We pulled out our speakers and a chair for Kaweah to sit in the back of the truck, Kaweah looked like the queen of a parade. One microphone set up for Kaweah, and another microphone was stretched out for me the driver. Before we got started, I called and asked Theresa, "Would you or Pastor Grove like to ride with us in the parade?" Theresa said, "I'll call you back," the Holy Spirit was surely taking them out of their comfort zone, including Pastor's Groves ducks.

We lined up for the parade, classic car after classic car; hundreds of them were lined up. Then there we were; with our Mission America trailer wrapped with the words, "Our Hope Jesus Christ!" As we were preparing and waiting in line for the parade, I looked up, what a treat it was to see Pastor Grove and his beautiful wife, Bev walking towards us. They looked a little nervous, I think they were surprised we were in the parade, I said, "Pastor Grove if you like, you can ride in the front seat."

The parade started, Kaweah started singing patriotic songs from her CD, Our Liberty, including "God Bless America." As we drove down the street; both sides of the road were lined with people. I was sorry, I didn't have my camera on me, what a sight, we must have driven through a crowd of about 10,000 people. I could see a spark of hope and joy in the people who were Christian; they would give us the thumbs up, as our Mission America trailer went by. In some areas, the crowd would go wild and clap, as Kaweah boldly sang, "God Bless America."

Jill and Beverly walked behind the trailer, passing out over 2,000 fliers, they were running out fast, and of course, I had a microphone. I welcomed everybody to The Hope Center, Sunday morning, and to come to the Revival Meeting, "You don't want to miss it." In the midst of all those classic cars, Jesus was lifted up and He always has dominion. We were taking dominion of the city of Billings for the glory of God; and we had barely just begun.

The following days we passed out fliers and then the first Sunday service came, Kaweah sang, and I shared about Mission America. Pastor Grove preached and shared about Mission America. Pastor Grove smiled as he told his congregation, "I like my ducks in a row, yet Dr. Luauna, and the Mission America team they are not only taking my ducks out of a row, they are taking me out of my comfort zone." Everyone laughed; Pastor Grove then shared about the upcoming meeting. We had four more days to finish blanketing the city with fliers and posters. Everyday our team was up early for prayer, then out to blanket the city for five hours, with hundreds of posters and a map of the city of Billings in hand.

On Labor Day, we labored! Since we discovered how convenient it was to set up the microphone and place a speaker in the back of the truck, after all we were a driving billboard. We drove from park to park, shopping mall to shopping mall announcing our revival meeting. The response from the people was amusing, as they looked all around trying to figure out where the voice was coming from; then they would see the trailer, "Our Hope, Jesus Christ!" It is always fun and adventurous laboring in the Kingdom of God, there is never a dull moment.

On Wednesday night Pastor Grove, asked me to preach at the Montana Rescue Mission, there were about 30 to 40 men throughout the building. As I looked around, I knew many of these men had given a dull ear to the gospel. The Holy Spirit stirred like a fire in my heart saying, "You shall never see them again; preach it straight." That's just what I did, the uncut, unadulterated Word of God. I shared my story, preached and gave the altar call. Nine men answered the call that night; I encouraged them to be in the meetings at The Hope Center. There was excitement in the air; the Holy Spirit was working on hearts. As we walked out the door, Pastor Grove asked, "Did I get a sample of your preaching?" I smiled and said, "Paul said I become all things to all men. Don't worry; I don't preach that direct, but these guys needed it."

The following day the three day meeting was to begin, the team went out early every morning while I prayed and prepared for the meeting. The first night of the meeting finally arrived, and we were ready for action, prayed up and read up. We arrived at the church at 4:30 pm for prayer; another group came to pray at 6:00 p.m. The first night nine people came forward to answer the altar call for salvation, there were about six others who raised their hands for salvation but did not come forward with the other nine. The Holy Spirit was working in the hearts of the people.

Throughout the three nights it was amazing, every night the crowd grew, 70 people were saved, and about 20 people were filled with the Holy Spirit. The Holy Spirit added new believers to the church every night. What a joy, to see each person come to Jesus, a man named Dennis, a tall Indian man, recommitted his life back to Christ. Now with a purpose and a destiny to live for, Jesus makes all the difference.

There were many healings throughout those three services. On Friday night, a lady came to church with a broken toe and three jammed toes on the same foot. During the altar call, she was helping to pray for others, she did not ask for prayer for herself. When she left the church, she was walking to the car and realized her toes did not hurt anymore. She could not wait to tell us she was healed when she came the next night.

Another woman was experiencing pain in her hip and on her left side from a previous car accident; on Friday night, during the music, she felt God's healing touch and the pain stopped, she was healed. Another woman had continual stomach pain and she was also healed on Friday night, this does not include all of the spiritual healings which took place.

I love this church, I knew from the first time I met Pastor Grove, we had a kindred spirit, when he shared with me about a vision for a facility called, "Hope House," it stirred my heart. I knew God had a bigger plan! God's desire is to fill "Hope House" with hundreds of men and women for discipleship; whose lives will be changed for eternity. This is just the beginning for The Hope Center, God is building an army of men and women who will be faithful, obedient, and filled with Holy Ghost power! God is doing something powerful in this church in Billings, Montana.

What a privilege and honor to be just a little part of what God is doing in His church, I am humbled and honored to have had an opportunity to be used by God in Billings, Montana. At The Hope Center, eyes have not seen, ears have not heard, neither has it entered into their hearts all the things that God has prepared for them who love Him and trust Him and are called according to His purpose. Pastor Grove and his wife, Bev are true shepherds.

I noticed how wonderful it is when we found a church that prays, and are led by the Holy Spirit, we see doors open. My desire is to always work with a local church in the area where our Mission America Team labors, why? Because as we win hundreds of souls throughout America, we hope to see each new believer continue their growth in God, and a local church is where the Holy Spirit finishes His work. I am saved to save. I am also called to help the body of Christ, to help leaders grow and become stronger in Jesus. I know my calling, I love people and I love His church.

Pastor Grove, his wife Bev, and The Hope Center will forever be deep in my heart, this is a new start for this wonderful church. At the end of our three day meeting, Pastor Grove with a humble heart, announced, "I was spiritually starving inside and I know I was doing better than most people here. We have been touched in a special way." As I listened I wanted to weep, because I knew right then, that was why the Holy Spirit did not allow us to leave Billings, Montana. God's love for this church, and these people, touched the very heartbeat of the Master.

I pray everyday and ask, "Holy Spirit lead us to the cities and the pastors, who are crying out in prayer, those who are open to the Holy Spirit, His servant, and the Mission America Team."

__Matthew 9:37-38__, "Then He said to His disciples, 'The harvest truly is plentiful, but the laborers are few. Therefore pray the Lord of the harvest to send out laborers into His harvest."

The King is coming for His Church; we must labor while we have time. Praise God for the Holy Spirit who leads us and directs our path. At the end of our meeting at The Hope Center, we were all rejoicing and praising God for He had done glorious things in our midst!

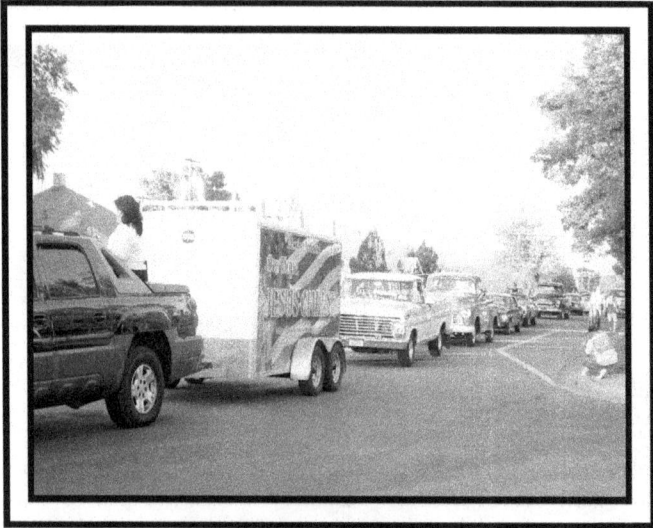

Parade in Billings

Bev & Pastor Grove

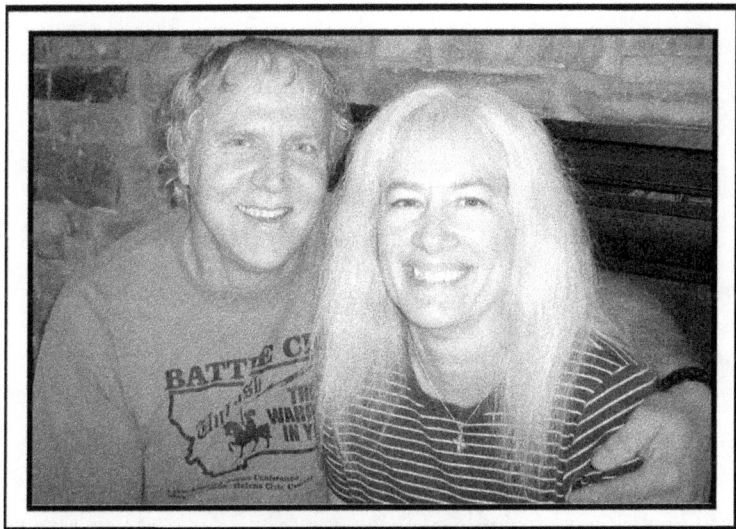

Chip & Diane Crees

Chapter Seventeen
Mission America Journey

My Birthplace

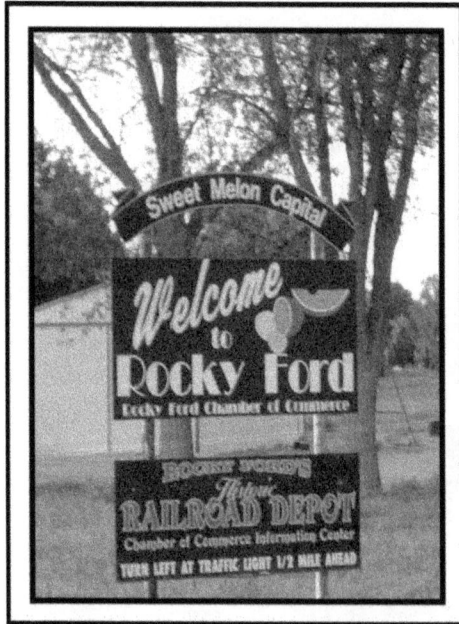

*T*he Holy Spirit had placed in my heart to go back to the place of my birth for several years now, we were *actually headed on the road to Ordway and Rocky Ford. It is amazing, how God orders our steps, our times and seasons are truly in His hands. I honestly was not sure what to expect next.*

I called around and found there was a KOA Campground in La Junta, Colorado, We would be driving through Rocky Ford, the place of my birth and passing Ordway, where my grandpa lived many years before. The road was a rural highway; many improvements had been made since my last trip back home. Although, the sun had set, the landmarks were unmistakable, signs distinctly marking the home of the world famous "Rocky Ford Melon!" We passed the road sign for Swink, "Wink and you'll miss it," the small town sandwiched between Rocky Ford and La Junta. Then we arrived at the KOA campground, unloaded and settled in for the night.

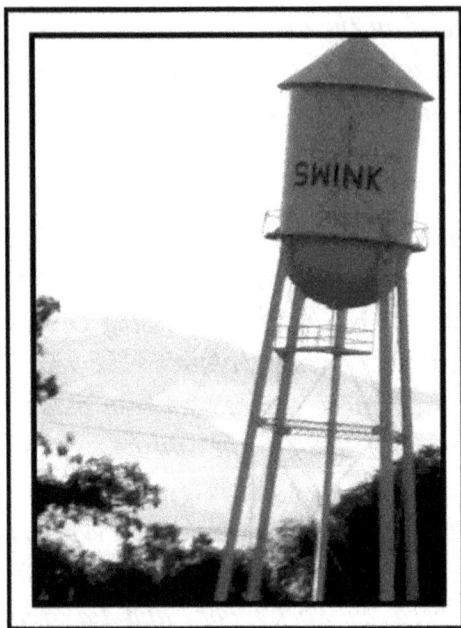

The next day, we rested before our next adventure. My aunt and cousin lived nearby in my grandpa's old house in Ordway, which was a drive over the train tracks into a different part of the countryside. I was prompted to look for a church in the area to have a revival in; after all, this was my old stomping grounds. As I've learned on this trip, to seek the Lord for direction, He has been faithful to lead us by His Spirit every step of the way. My aunt and cousin invited us over for lunch; they worked very hard and prepared some good old Colorado style Mexican food, there is nothing like home cooking. We had a great time of fellowship, sharing photo albums, memories and enjoying the company of family.

Next we went driving around with my cousin to spy out the land, she wanted to introduce me to a pastor she knew in the city. Several weeks before we arrived, I called the pastor and sent information ahead to give him advance notice and information. We went to the church and talked with the pastor, he was a young man, as many pastors do he works a second full time job. We talked, I explained we have been traveling across the United States, evangelizing in different cities and working with local pastors to bring in a harvest of souls. We would do all of the outreach, provide the fliers and do all the promotion of the event. He said he would think about it, talk to his Board members and call me the next day. When we left his house, I asked my cousin if she knew of any other locations for a revival meeting, any other church buildings, community centers or empty store fronts. We drove by a few locations, made contacts, and ended up at a realtor's office. The afternoon was fading away and we started back to the KOA cabin to walk the little missionary puppies.

This is the point in the mission where I press in through prayer. The Lord has been guiding us every step of the way, He led us to strategic cities, churches, roads, gas stations, restaurants, and even sidewalks. I had to hear His voice clearly, because we were in Colorado in September, I knew from my experience living here how the weather conditions could change fast. I did not want to drive the truck and trailer in bad weather. What should we do?

After we took care of the little dogs, we headed up the road to Rocky Ford; I wanted to take pictures of the signs. We drove around and stumbled upon the hospital I was born in, I went inside, and then back outside to take more pictures. It was getting dark and we hadn't eaten dinner yet.

We were all undecided what we wanted to eat; I did not want to just drive around so I pulled into the parking lot of a Mexican restaurant on the main street. We sat in the car still deciding what to do, the question was, "Do we eat here or go somewhere else? If not here, where?" It was one of those kind of conversations; I asked the girls, "Do you want to eat here?" They each answered, "It doesn't matter to me, do you want to eat here?" Then I said, "I don't know. Where else could we go?" Did we want to drive through a fast food restaurant and take the food back to the cabin? Then I looked around the parking lot, I try not to eat at restaurants where the parking lot is empty at dinner time, scary. Well, there were cars and an older couple just parked and was walking inside, I rolled down the window and asked, "Is the food good here?" They answered, "Yeah, we like it." Ok, somebody make a decision, let's go in!

The nights were cool, the girls had on their Mission America T-shirts and their Mission America sweat jackets; we were definitely a walking advertisement and everywhere we went people took notice. We were ambassadors for Jesus Christ; His name was clearly displayed on our "uniform". We sat down and looked over the menu, Jill and Beverly went for the menudo. As we were sitting in the booth, I told the girls, "Maybe I missed it this time, if God doesn't open the door for a revival meeting; we should pack up and head on the road. We should be heading back home soon." During dinner, I noticed a nice looking couple sitting in the booth behind us; they kept looking at the back of our sweat jackets; we have learned that our mission statement makes some people happy and others not.

The man was dressed in the local fashion, after all this was cowboy country; he had a black cowboy hat, black leather vest and cowboy boots. As they stood up to leave the restaurant, he came over to our booth and asked, "What exactly is Mission America?" All along our travels, we were asked the same question; it is always a question which holds opportunity for witnessing and giving glory to Jesus.

I began to explain, and to share that I was born in Rocky Ford; I thought the Lord wanted me to hold a revival to reach my family and the community since my life had been totally transformed by the power of God. When I was finished, I asked for his name, he said, "My name is Pastor Rex, I just took over as pastor at the local Assembly of God Church here in Rocky Ford." He gave me his card and we just so happened to leave all our fliers in the truck. Jill didn't waste any time, she jumped up, went to the truck and brought some fliers in.

She said to Pastor Rex, "It cannot be a coincidence that we've traveled thousands of miles across the U.S. to Rocky Ford, to have a revival and we run into you." He and his wife were very sweet and kind, he sounded interested, yet he asked me to call him the next day.

I don't know how long we were dragging our feet in the parking lot, in the natural it probably looked and sounded ridiculous, debating over where to have dinner. Yet in the supernatural, I can just imagine the haggling between the little angel sitting on my right shoulder whispering, "Go inside," and the little devil whispering on the left shoulder,

213

"Leave," in these seemingly insignificant decisions, the Lord is directing our paths for a greater destination and purpose.

Although the evening ended on a positive note by meeting Pastor Rex and his wife, we still did not have a definite plan or schedule for revival. We needed an answer, the first pastor never called, so I called him. He said, he had to decline our offer because he had to work and the board members were not interested either. Ok, no problem, no offense, that meant we weren't supposed to be there.

Instead of calling Pastor Rex, I was compelled to stop by the church. Jill and I found him inside the church building, we talked at length and had the kinship feeling we get with fellow Christians and like-minded pastors who have the same vision for the harvest. Finally, I told him, we do not expect, nor ask anything of him or the church. We will do all the work; we will create, print and pay for the fliers. He said, he was praying and the Lord told him for October to be a time of witnessing, soul winning and inviting people to church, the last Sunday service he made his announcement; then we showed up. The revival was scheduled for the beginning of October.

Pastor Rex had just taken over the church and in this rural community, there were the faithful, long time members, but he was ready to bring in a harvest of new souls. We went to work right away, Pastor Rex provided a nice wooden board and helped me construct a sign for the driveway of the church, using the banners which were provided by The Hope Center, Theresa made it possible for us to reuse them for other cities as well. I contacted the local media; mostly rural newspapers with a press release and interviews; they were willing to cover the story and ran the press release ahead of the revival. Jill, Beverly and Kaweah hit the streets, hanging posters in every business and light pole in the town; they also went door to door in the neighborhoods.

Expectation was in the air for the first night of the revival; I was excited as my family came in the doors, my aunt and cousin, they brought some friends with them each night. The church began to fill up; a young lady less than five feet tall walked in, she was the manager at the Sonic Burger on the main street. Kaweah had invited her and her co-worker to come to the meetings and they both came the first night and gave their hearts to the Lord. I think Pastor Rex was surprised by all the new visitors who were coming in the doors; he was ready for a revival. Couples came who had not been going to church; whole families came from the surrounding communities including La Junta. Each night the services were full; many of the people came every night.

I watched Pastor Rex, I knew he was serious about soul winning; he had ushers ready at the door with new visitor cards, after the service he collected the cards treating them as new found treasures for God's kingdom. I also saw him minister with all his heart to every single person who walked through the doors and during the altar call; he truly has a shepherd's heart. Then he took a whole crew out for a meal and fellowship after each service; he was breaking bread as they did in the Book of Acts.

The last day of the revival was on Sunday; we had services in the morning and the evening. An older gentleman walked in who had been invited from the door-to-door outreach; the power of God touched him in a special way, he left with tears in his eyes and said he was grateful that we came to his door, he lives alone and his family lives far away. Sunday night, he returned in the evening for the last service and tried to take us out for dinner.

As we had lunch with Pastor Rex and Debbie; I saw a new spark in his eye and sensed a new fire in his spirit; he talked about having his own t-shirts made and taking a team like ours to spread the gospel in his county; he proudly called it, "Mission Otero!" God certainly ordered our footsteps; it was a Divine Appointment to meet this awesome couple in my birthplace. As I listened to their entire testimony I know, Jesus has a very special assignment for them; they have been faithful over the little and God will give them much!

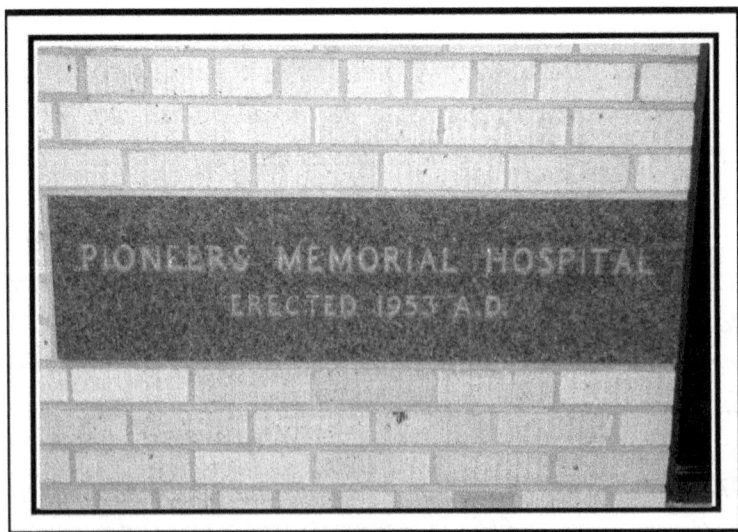

Pastor Rex & Debbie

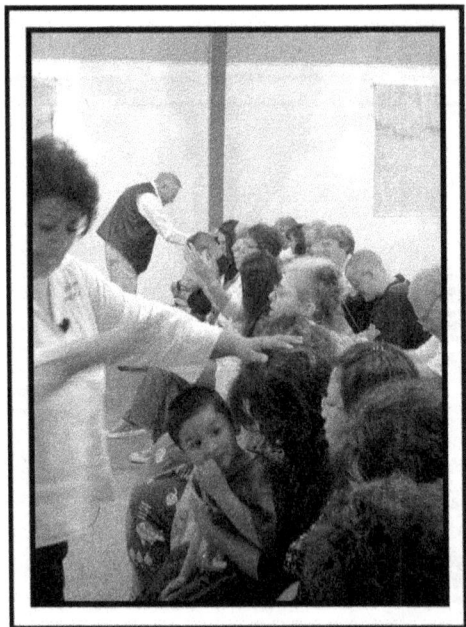

When God Takes You Full Circle

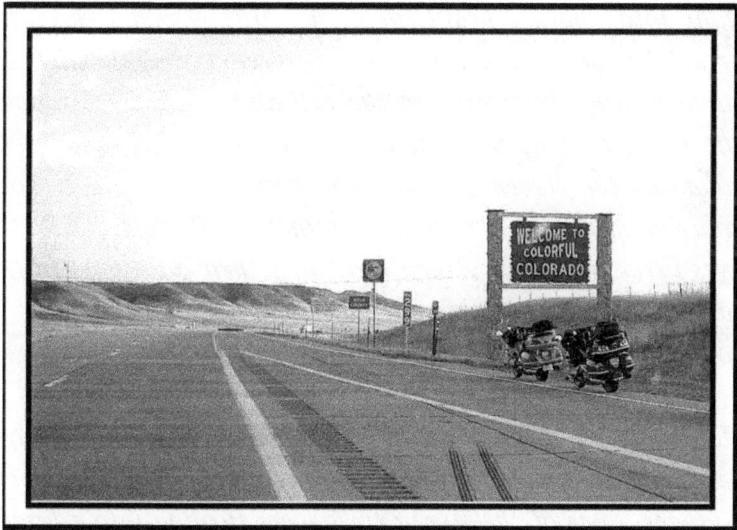

*W*ow, what an amazing God we serve! Our second Mission America trip has been just amazing; we have been busy for Jesus, non stop. We traveled from one place to another, a million thoughts passed through my mind, which is when I wish I had a tape recorder in hand, not wanting to miss one thought.

It had been many years since I had been back to Colorado, I remembered preaching my mother's funeral, and later sharing at Beverly's father's memorial service.

How can I find words to describe the beautiful scenery before my eyes? As my mind searches for just the right words to describe and share even just a glimpse of these majestic views of the Colorado Rocky Mountains. Driving over the pass, the mountains were covered with so many different colors, fire orange, red and yellow, an artist or cameraman's dream I am sure. With each turn one view ran right into another beautiful view. The Aspen trees were breathtaking, as the green leaves were saying goodbye to summer, and welcoming in the fall and winter. I stopped the truck to take a moment to soak in those bright, gold colors of the Aspen leaves; they were like shiny new gold coins dangling on a thousand branches. Then I closed my eyes listening as the Aspen trees sing their own song in the wind, as each tree sings in harmony with one another, a song only heard in the Rocky Mountains of Colorado.

As we got closer to the top of the mountain 13,000 feet the temperature was colder, and with cold comes more color changes, some of the Aspen trees were turning into a bright rust color, soon to be screaming bright red. Again, my breath was taken away with this amazing beauty, far beyond what one could really describe in words, unless they have been right where I stood. These Colorado mountains are amazing, midnight and indigo blue, only the ungodly would say there is no God after seeing His Mighty workmanship, His wonder is seen everywhere I look in these Colorado Mountains.

We arrived in Silverthorne, after driving through Dillon, Colorado, and at the best time of the year, wow! I knew the team needed a few days rest, a decision was made to camp in Silverthorne at Columbine Landing, it is hidden away in the crevices of the mountains right beside the Blue River. We thought maybe three or four days after all who could resist these beautiful, colorful Rocky Mountains? We unpacked our tents, set up camp, and I saw my fishing pole in close reach, I knew this was God's blessing from all our labor.

The sound of the river flowing never seems to run dry, day or night, as the river dances over rocks and boulders, its white waves of rushing water as they crash against the rocks, and then all of a sudden you notice in another area, the river is so clean you can see the bottom of the riverbed.

This freezing clear water is so refreshing and comforting, what a glorious place to unwind after 17 days of working in the harvest field. Now a few days to rest, then our Mission America team will launch out on the road again. As my mind unwinds, knowing the girls truly need a few days with no phones, no computer, just this beauty that is set before my eyes by God Almighty. Soaking in every change of the sky as the sun goes down behind the mountain and the comfort of the campfire in the night to keep warm, and of course the beauty of the rising sun as it creeps over the mountain wows my heart.

As I sit down on the edge of the river with my fishing pole, I am taken way back in time when my children were only 7 years old and up into their teen years. How we used to camp in these Rocky Mountains it was a way of life for our family, as they were growing up. Where did all those years go? Years have gone by, from the time we left Colorado; my son was only a teenager the last time we fished together in these Colorado Rivers. He now fishes with his sons, Josh and Zack. My daughter Kaweah, who never liked to fish, always seemed to bring a book as she sat on a rock reading, while my son Sam and I fished the river. Or she would stay back at camp with the tent and those who just enjoyed sitting around the campfire. Then Sam and I would walk the river, knowing we would find just the right place to pull out that prize trout, one we were sure we would mount on the wall above the fireplace. We never did catch that prize fish, but we did capture memories that will forever be etched in my mind.

After all those years passed, there I was on our Mission America trip, my daughter Kaweah 33 years old, turns to me and says, "Mom, maybe I will try fishing." What a surprise, I let her know I was ready to teach her. I pulled out my extra fishing rod, of course I always keep on hand, after all you never know while traveling when the opportunity might arise and you get a chance to try the river. This was one of those special moments the river is calling, I asked Kaweah, "Are you ready for fishing 101?"

What fun, did we catch any fish? No, only a tiny, baby trout, four inches long. We laughed as I gently released him, and said, "Maybe next year we shall see you again, you're free little fishy, swim away."

Well, the first night temperatures dropped, brrrr, we all froze, dogs included. We woke and hurried to bundle up with extra sweaters and jackets, the morning was cold, 39 degrees. I thought, "What is this?" In the past it did not get cold until the end of October, this was September. After a camp breakfast, we headed into town to find a thrift store to find some extra blankets to throw over our sleeping bags, and a few for the missionary puppies. The second night, brrrr, again the temperatures dropped to 37 degrees. As I stood outside the tent, I looked at the girls, and laughed, we were all freezing, I looked up at the clouds and suddenly remembered, "Girls, those are snow clouds!" We smiled, and almost at once we said, "Pack it up! Enough of this Colorado camping, let's head to Colorado Springs, and get a warm motel." Within a few hours, we were packed. Did I forget to share it rained the night before, and water was misting inside the tent. I looked to Kaweah, and asked, "I thought you waterproofed the tent before we left California." She smiled and said, "I did, but only the seams!" Oops! I placed a tarp on top of the tent, but it stopped raining by the time I got it covered. After the rain, the winds blew 30 to 40 miles an hour, our tarp blew frantically throughout the whole night, along with the howling wind. I think we were ready for a motel. But we did have fun and had a good laugh in the midst of all the beauty.

We arrived in Colorado Springs and we found a nice warm motel room. The next day as we went outside, I looked towards the mountains I saw snow. We just missed one foot of snow, thank you Jesus for wisdom.

We made contact with an old friend and I was set up to minister for the next Sunday services. As I prepared for both of Sunday's meetings, we called a few people we knew; it would be wonderful to see old friends. I ministered under the power of the Holy Spirit, I could feel this church needed a new fresh touch from Jesus. Many people had been wounded, and it lingered in the air.

How great it was to see Pastor Mark Garcia and Debbie, they were long ago friends. What a blessing to see him now the pastor of his own church, I know God has a plan for this couple, they have been faithful. The time we were able to spend in fellowship was truly a gift. Time and dates did not allow for a three day meeting in their church, but in those two meetings the Holy Spirit moved in His power, the altars were filled, and healing came from the Master Himself. People were saved that morning in both services. We left their service, and were happy with everything the Lord did in a short time.

Brrrrr

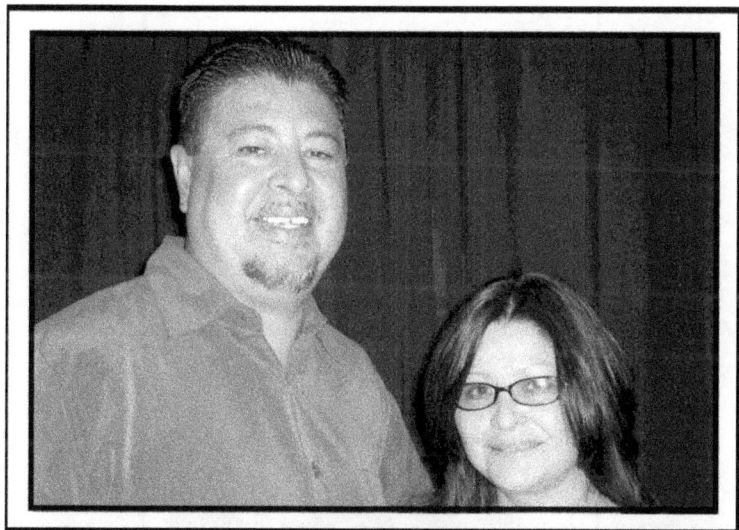

Pastor Mark & Debbie Garcia

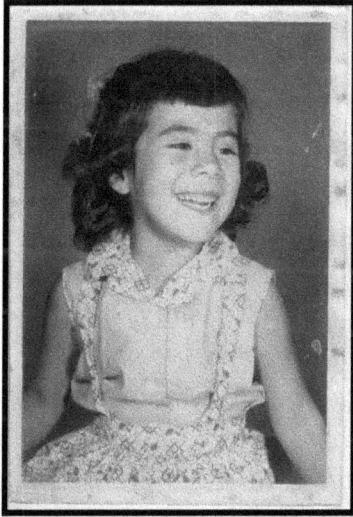
Dr. Luauna as a young girl

The next day we spent some time praying for the Holy Spirit to guide us to the next place, our desire was to be where He wanted us. That was more important than anything in the world, so into prayer we went, I remembered Pastor Mark, from the church we just left, told me of an old friend of ours who had a church in Pueblo, Colorado. Beverly found his number, and I made the call. I left a message and within ten minutes, Pastor Darin returned my call, I shared about Mission America, and I could tell he was somewhat open, but I felt by the Holy Spirit he was worried about monies. I said, "Let's meet for coffee." We had to drive through his town anyway; he agreed but wanted to call his wife Gloria to let her know.

Well, on the road towards Pueblo, Colorado my phone rang but I did not hear it, I forgot to take it off silence. Later, I realized there was a missed call, I checked the message, and *was surprised to hear Pastor Darin, say, "No, maybe another time." As I finished listening to the message, I felt the Holy Spirit speak to my heart, "Do not call him back, nor agree with his decision," I thought that was strange, normally I would just continue on.*

Thinking and praying, "Lord, how do I do this?" I waited until we arrived in Pueblo, and ignored the fact that Pastor Darin had told us to go on, he said maybe next time when we are in the area. I called Pastor Darin's answering machine the second time, I told him, "We are now in Pueblo, and waiting to meet you, let's have coffee and of course a bowl of Colorado green chile." Pastor Darin, called back and again tried to say not right now, right at that same moment, again the Holy Spirit spoke to my heart, "Meet him in person." I said, "Listen, Pastor Darin, its lunch time, you need to eat, we need to eat, let's at least meet for lunch," he hesitated but finally agreed. I did not know what the Holy Spirit had in mind, but I knew it was something more than my eyes or mind could comprehend.

We found the restaurant; and arriving first we got a table and sat down. I prayed, "Lord, give me wisdom when Pastor Darin comes, help me see with your eyes, and hear with your ears." As I finished praying, Pastor Darin walked in with two other men, I stood, and gave him a hug. Wow, this man was a different man, changed by the power of the Holy Spirit. My mind went back in time for a moment, 27 years ago when this man, was a hard core drug addict, his beautiful wife Gloria was in my women's home. He was facing prison, so filled with hate and bitterness, now he was changed and filled with the Holy Spirit. As I shared our vision and the things the Lord was doing, tears came to his eyes, I knew right then the Lord had a great plan. I told Pastor Darin, we did not come for money; I came to be a blessing.

Right then his wife walked in the door, she was just as beautiful now as 27 years ago. She was so sweet; we stood and said our, "hellos," and shared back and forth all the Lord was doing in both of our lives. What a blessing, just sitting at this table sharing God's amazing grace in the lives of this couple was worth it all. Then Pastor Darin turned around and said to the two guys with him, "Pastor Luauna told me twenty seven years ago, God had a plan for my life, and this trouble will all pass. She told me one day, God will use you to preach the gospel." He shared with them, "I was so mad when Pastor Luauna told me that back then, and look, now I am a preacher." We both had tears in our eyes; God was knitting our hearts in a very special way. I was so proud of Pastor Darin & Gloria, I did not care if we had a three day meeting or not, just having this time at lunch was a blessing. Then just like that, Pastor Darin turned to his wife and said, "I changed my mind. We are going to have a three day meeting, I know its God." We all smiled at each other, I asked, "So where is your church?" I wanted to get the address so I could get some fliers done fast.

Pastor Darin then went on to tell me how God opened the door for him to have his church in an old orphanage building. Right then my heart skipped a beat! I looked into his eyes and said, "Is it the old Sacred Heart Orphanage?" He was surprised, and answered, "Yes." Wow, I told him I was in that same orphanage as a child, immediately I knew

231

without a doubt, God was going to do something more than I could even imagine. Many years ago, I remember asking my mother about that old building, she told me it had been knocked down. All of those years I thought the building was no longer in existence. Now by God's amazing grace I find out it has not been torn down at all. Years later, I would return to the Sacred Heart Orphanage and preach in the very same building.

Plans were made and the meeting was set up, after lunch Pastor Darin asked if I wanted to see the church. We agreed and followed him to the church. As we drove up towards the entrance, I suddenly went back to yesteryear, the old rock walls awakened some old memories, long ago forgotten. As we drove into the parking lot, a thousand memories went through my mind, like an old movie, one frame at a time; rolling through my mind, I was not sure what I was going to feel.

As I wandered throughout that old brick building, I was astonished, as I remembered so many things I thought I forgot. As I walked up and down those halls, the little girl who once cried herself to sleep every night was now all grown up. I ran my hands along the walls and up the old wooden carved banister stair rails, like I did as a child. I climbed each floor as an adult remembering the very foot prints I made as a child. I noticed the tile floors were still the same with their tiny ceramic squares, up and down each hall.

Then we walked into the little church, funny as a child it seemed so much bigger, I remembered walking down the very same aisle, the only difference, the wooden floors were now replaced with carpet and the old statues throughout the church were now gone. I walked to the front, turned left and walked down in front of the very same wooden pew I sat in as a child. Sitting down right in the same spot I was made to sit as a little girl, my eyes staring from one side of the platform looking around the whole church until I covered every inch of that room.

I remembered services as a child in this building, at one point thinking God must hate me that's why my mother left me in this place. As I sat thinking of all the silent tears and cries that must be hidden away in the walls of this old building, as thousands of young children were rejected by their mothers and fathers, hearts so broken, filled with rejection and anger. This very same building, had become a place of redemption, freedom, joy, and victory, where life is given back to the broken hearted, and healing is brought to the oppressed.

As I sat looking and thinking, I smiled inside, wondering what was God's plan for bringing me back to this place, He has brought me around full circle. My thoughts were interrupted, as Pastor Darin had to get back to work, and we needed to get everything ready for the meetings.

We prepared fliers and the team worked hard to blanket the area, starting around the old orphanage, and working their way out into the city. Banners and fliers were placed on hundreds of street corners, inviting people to come and hear the powerful story. Little did the people know how this was one miraculous story of God's amazing grace! Three days went by, and the first night had finally come, the Holy Spirit was wonderful in our midst, His power touched deep into the hearts of the men and women present, Jesus was ready to heal and save. The altar was filled, and His love touched each person as they wept and cried out to the Master.

More and more people arrived at the service each night, and without fail the Holy Spirit met us each night, people being saved, healed, and filled with their prayer language. Pastor Darin and Pastor Gloria, were touched in a powerful way as well, they are so special. As I watched the Lord fill the church with His glory, I knew the Lord had a mighty plan for this couple.

I will call this couple "One in a Million," they are a true work of God's mighty hand. Each night was more powerful than the night before, and by the last night the church was filled with new wonderful people. Heaven was rejoicing as people were brought into the Kingdom of God.

As I ministered, the Holy Spirit placed on my heart to tell one couple, "This is the church you are supposed to be in." I thought it strange, because I never tell people what church to attend. Again, this came to my heart the second time I looked at this couple. Finally after the third time I said, "Ok, Holy Spirit!" I walked up to them as they sat close to the front row I looked right into their eyes, and said, "This is the church you are supposed to be in!" As I finished saying those words the woman took a deep breath, and covered her mouth in surprise. I walked away not knowing she had told the Holy Spirit earlier, "If you want us in this church, please tell us tonight!" Well, the Holy Spirit, knew where they needed to be, and answered their question. Just ask Jesus, He is faithful!

Sunday morning service arrived and more new people came into the little church in the orphanage. As I ministered, I noticed two strong, distinguished looking men, sitting in the back row. I gave the altar call, and they both raised their hands to receive Jesus. As people came forward, the Holy Spirit put such compassion in my heart for these two brothers, I spoke out, "You have been rejected, and Jesus wants to bring healing." I went back to pray for them, and I could see tears in their eyes. One of the men asked, "Do you remember us? We were in this orphanage at the same time you were here."

I looked at them and searched my memory, although their eyes looked familiar. As a little girl, I was so broken and scared; I asked their names, they sounded familiar. As we talked after the service, one of the brothers said, "I became a Christian, and my wife as well, she was a special lady." Yet, the other brother who had just prayed to receive Jesus that morning, I could see he still needed healing from the hurts of yesteryear, he was still broken inside. I reached out and touched his shoulder, and looked him right in the eyes and said, "Jesus loves you, and you are so special!" He could not keep my eye contact; he lowered his eyes to the floor. I remembered what it was like years back to think I was anything but good, let alone thinking that Jesus loved me. I will pray for this special man, and in time I know healing will come to his heart.

As the revival was coming to a close on the last night, a young lady came in named Andronica. As I ministered I could see right through her life, she was broken, wounded, and abused. This woman sat right in the very seat I sat as a child, listening to the whole service, tears welling up in her eyes; yet she was fighting back the tears. Jesus longed to heal her broken heart. I called her forward, and shared with her, "Jesus loves you and He has a wonderful plan for your life, do not hide behind drugs and alcohol, Jesus wants to heal the hurt of your heart."

As I reached out to lay hands on her, she started to weep like a child; the Holy Spirit was bringing healing to her heart. I reached out and hugged her with all my might, as she wept like a baby. I remembered all those years back, I just needed someone to tell me Jesus loved me. She was so touched, and she was filled with the Holy Spirit, she began to speak in other tongues. The power from on high showered her, with His amazing grace, love and power for her tomorrows.

The night before, the Holy Spirit placed on my heart, there was a couple in the service who needed healing from a broken heart because of an unexpected death of a loved one. A couple came forward, I could see the pain surrounding them, and I just wanted to weep with them. As I laid hands on them, I felt the healing salve of heaven come down upon them, the Bible says joy comes in the morning. No more pain, what the devil thought for bad God will use for good. I did not know they lost a daughter 25 years old; the pain of her death had overwhelmed them. The very next morning, our last day before leaving Pueblo, Colorado I wanted to get pictures of the old building. Once again, I ran into this wonderful couple, they were now shining with the light of Jesus. Healing did come in the morning, they are so special!

So many more people were touched in so many ways, old friends we came in contact with again; too many to list here. I almost forgot my old friend named Max, now married to his beautiful wife Margie. Max's daughter Tina lived with me when she was a child for about a year, and hung around my house for many years, like my second daughter, now all grown up. She and Kaweah were best friends, what a treat to see them once again. They will forever have a special place deep in my heart. So many old friends, it was like years were never an issue, the love of Jesus keeps our hearts afresh and new.

As I left the building that last day, I stood in the parking lot in the back of the building by my car door, looking over that old building before leaving. As I stood there looking, I felt like the Holy Spirit showed me a picture in my mind of a runner as they run across the finish line, hands lifted up, and chest forward. The Holy Spirit was saying to my heart, "Look, where I have brought you from, I planted little seeds in your heart as a child, now they are full grown, look at the victory, we have won! What the devil thought for bad, God has turned for good!"

The Holy Spirit spoke right to my heart, "You have My approval, you are My servant, and I am your Heavenly Father whom shall never leave you." I saw myself right then and there run through a yellow ribbon in my mind; I *lifted my hands high in the air in that parking lot, and shouted, "Rejection from a little girl is no more, it is finished!"*

What an awesome God we serve! Amen!

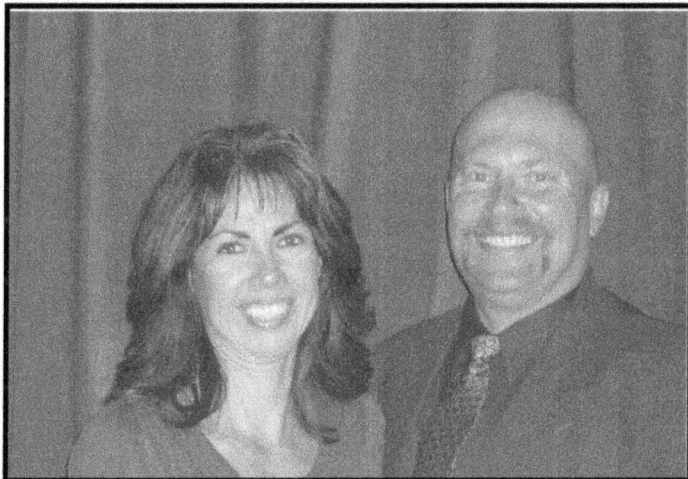

Pastors Darin & Gloria Carroll

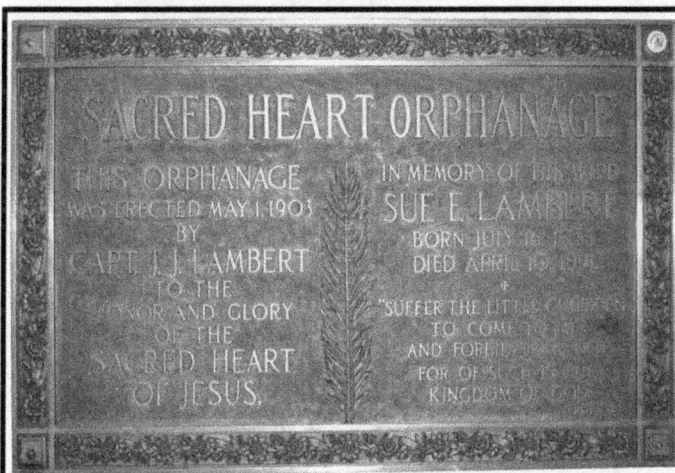

SACRED HEART ORPHANAGE

THIS ORPHANAGE
WAS ERECTED MAY 1, 1903
BY
CAPT. J. J. LAMBERT
TO THE
HONOR AND GLORY
OF THE
SACRED HEART
OF JESUS.

IN MEMORY OF HIS WIFE
SUE E. LAMBERT
BORN JULY 16, 1838
DIED APRIL 19, 1901

"SUFFER THE LITTLE CHILDREN
TO COME UNTO ME
AND FORBID THEM NOT
FOR OF SUCH IS THE
KINGDOM OF GOD."

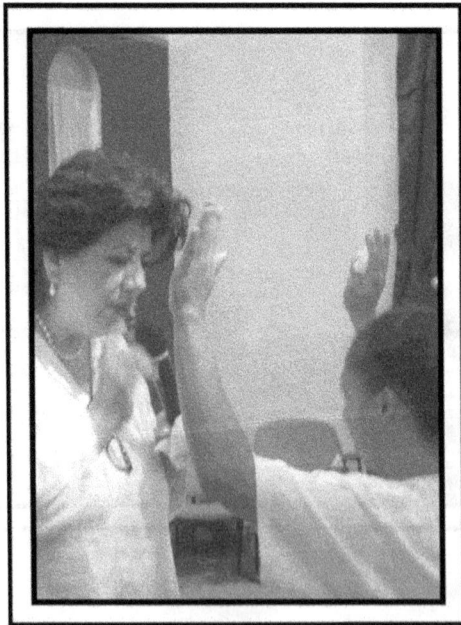

Our Mission does not end until Jesus calls His church up.
We shall be faithful laboring in the harvest field continuing

on our Mission from the Prayer Mountain in San Diego County and may He find us truly faithful.

> **_Psalm 126:6_**, "He who continually goes forth weeping, bearing seed for sowing, shall doubtless come again with rejoicing, bringing his sheaves with him."

Mission San Diego

S an Diego, what an amazing place, people from all over the world come to visit this city, known for the famous Sea World, San Diego Zoo, or Hotel Del Coronado. "The Del," this beachfront beauty that screams luxury, just across the San Diego Bay an amazing wooden Victorian resort, known as one of the oldest wooden buildings in California. It dates back to 1888, it's known for hosting presidents, and royalty, and of course movie stars from Hollywood, grace us with their presence.

San Diego with its beaches, cliffs, white sands, and of course let's not forget the early morning surfing done in La Jolla, and Mission Beach as hundreds gather. Then there is Balboa Park, with the world's largest Organ Pavilion, where concerts are heard in the summer nights, with music so sweet and beautiful it's whispered on the wings of the wind.

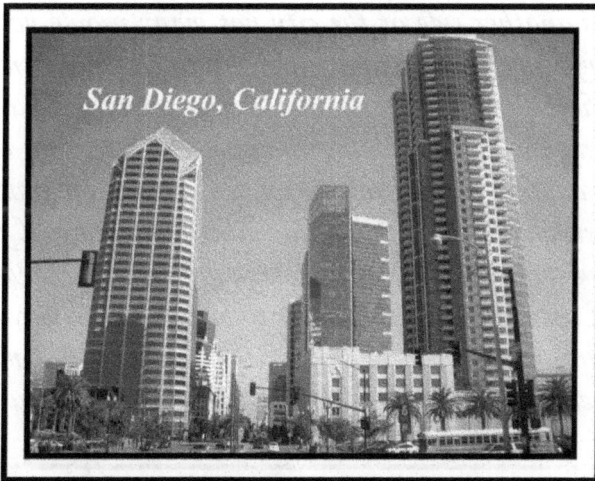
San Diego, California

The shores of San Diego, California with 70 miles of stunning beaches, where ships of every sort line the docks or shores, from the small private sail boats to family fishing boats, large cruise ships that dock to load and unload people from every corner of the world.

As they unload the people notice the breathtaking views of the city's high rise buildings, and just a few yards away the world's oldest active sailing ship graces the pier, with sails lifted and the hundreds of ropes throughout that great ship, as the tourists pull out their cameras to take home a picture of this 1863 Star of India ship.

Wow, the beauty is amazing throughout the city! No words can really describe the beauty. Only those who have come to this city can express what their eyes have seen. This perfect weather all year round, seems almost a perfect place!

Why Mission San Diego? *Behind all the beauty in this city there is another side of the city not many people notice. In the very same place tourist's line up to catch the trolley to visit the city, many do not notice the young girls who line up along the streets hoping to catch the attention of men, who would be willing to pay for sex. Under age prostitutes are everywhere throughout this city, while an evil force is busy working to smuggle underage girls across the Mexican border, some of these girls never to be seen again as young as 13 years of age. Where sexual abuse has pushed many of these teens into thinking, "What does it matter anyway?"*

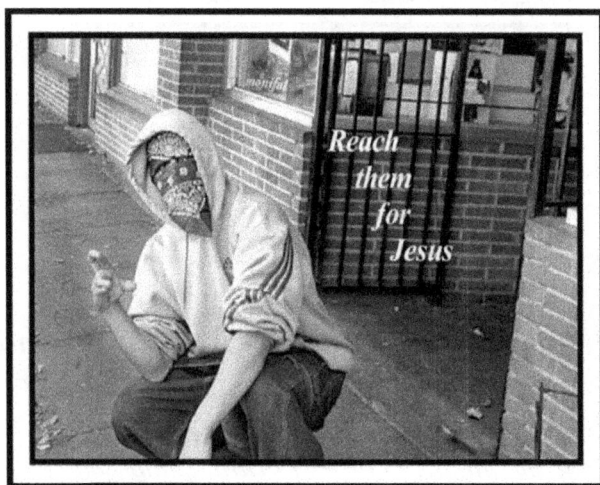

Also behind the walls of these beautiful homes are many broken hearts, fathers who are drunk, beating their wives in anger. Teens strung out on drugs, not just smoking pot, teens warm a spoon filled with powder to prepare a needle of this wicked substance called heroin.

Kids as young as 12, are playing Russian roulette with their lives, smoking crack that is so easy to access, the border of Mexico just 10 minutes away. There are so many family issues that cause many a teen to give into this demonic force of drug addiction, to hide the hurt and numb their heart. These teens only go deeper into a web of Satan, as John 10:10 comes alive, "The devil comes only but to kill steal and destroy!" Where there are very few places which take in these teens to help see them free. Parents are looking frantically to find help with their kid before they end up dead.

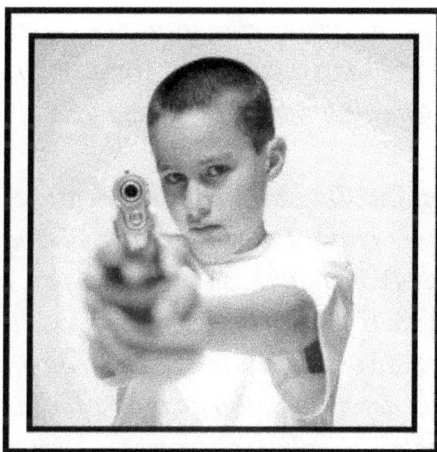

Why Mission San Diego? Wanting to reach out to the gay community with the gospel of hope, I set my camera up the first day of the Gay Pride Parade, to get film coverage for a documentary and a book I am writing, "It's Not Gay At All." I set my tripod and camera right in the middle of the street, one of the largest gay pride marches, known as the 5th largest celebration of gay pride in the United States, with over 165,000 people attending and marching. I think they thought I was part of a TV crew so no one bothered me as I was filming. I wanted to show what force was behind this march through film, only to discover I had to close my eyes as not to be defiled by what I was filming. Men and women, young and old, rich and poor, were marching, so blinded by this force behind the spirit of darkness. One of my helpers, in tears as she was shocked to see what was in front of us; I asked her if she was ok. She lowered her head in shame, as she said, "Why is the church not doing their job, reaching these people who are so lost?" Tears streaming down her face, I knew she had been behind the church walls for too long. San Diego, known as a gay hub, teens by the thousands are being swept into this lifestyle without warning of the destruction to come upon them. Why Mission San Diego? Because they need JESUS!

Why Mission San Diego? Mercedes, Bentleys, Jaguars and giant limousines cruise the streets approaching their million dollar homes. People with so much money in their bank accounts, yet their souls are empty, lost and bound by fear. Behind closed doors, many only spiral into the depths of oppression and depression. No amount of money can buy the peace that only comes from JESUS.

Bars along 5th Avenue filled with people looking to fill the void of their heart, going from one bar to another, one night stand after another, leaving them scarred by sin. Thousands of people up and down the streets, some businessmen and women so drunk they can barely walk to find their car. Staggering up and down the street, no different looking than the homeless person, whose eyes are so empty, when you look into them all you see is a void!

250

The homeless tent is set up only half a mile away, where over 3,000 homeless gather in hopes to find a bunk for the night, while people just feed their tummies and not their souls.

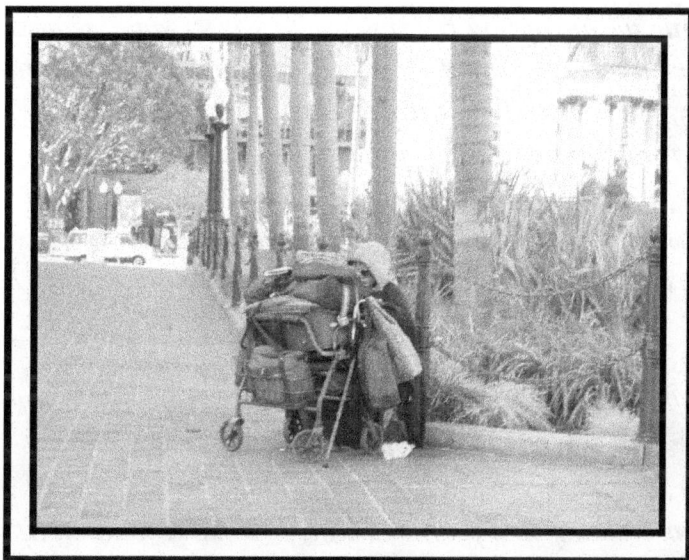

Driving along these beautiful streets, caught and swept away in it's beauty, one does not notice all the other homeless who gather along the freeways, or under the park benches, or in their cardboard boxes to sleep along the sidewalk, out of sight from all the tourists who flock to see this beautiful city, San Diego.

Why Mission San Diego? *The population in all of San Diego County is 3 million! Jesus looked at Jerusalem and He wept! I have not even touched on the gang violence, the hate that causes one group of people to kill another group of* people. San Diego, California is filled with gang violence; everyday someone is in the hospital or killed.

Why Mission San Diego? False religion is everywhere, while we are out on the trolley, the streets, and the buses, 5 -6 hours a day, three days a week reaching out to hundreds a day, we are not surprised to find other people passing out fliers and giving people poison.

False doctrine is given out on a silver platter, as the devil sweeps thousands into deception, thousands think they have the truth; while they walk in death, spiritual death. We must help them, we must bring them out of deception as well, and it is only the gospel of Jesus who will break the yoke.

I am trusting God for San Diego, to build the largest Spirit-filled Christian church full of the glory and power of the Almighty God. If God speaks to your heart to help, then please do so!

We have church services in the very heart of the city, for a Saturday 6 pm service, and on Wednesday a noon service right on the streets in the heart of the city of San Diego, Ca. This city shall be filled in the mighty name of Jesus Christ, with the GLORY of the Lord! Our goal: Fill the Prayer Mountain with new believers, souls won for the Glory of the Lord. Join us, and please pray for us. We also hold a service at the Prayer Mountain every Sunday at 10 am, and Wednesday at 7 pm. Thank you so much for your time! We are breaking through to new ground, taking back the land, to God be all the glory, and may God bless you! Remember, share Jesus everywhere you go, and when you stand on the other side. What a GREAT reward, people thanking you for telling them about the wonderful saving Grace of our Lord and Savior Jesus Christ.

Soldiers of Christ, arise,
and put your armor on;
Fight, for the battle will be ours;
we fight to win a crown.
We fight not against flesh,
We wrestle not with blood;
but principalities and powers,
and for the TRUTH of God.

Charles Wesley

At the sounding of the trumpet, when the saints are gathered home, we shall greet each other by the crystal sea; when the Lord Himself from heaven to His glory bids them come, what a gathering of the faithful that will be!

When the angel of the Lord proclaims that time shall be nor more, we shall gather, and the saved and ransomed see; then to meet again together, on the bright, celestial shore, what a gathering of the faithful that will be!

At the great and final judgment, when the hidden comes to light, when the Lord in all His glory we shall see; at the bidding of our Saviour, "Come, ye blessed, to My right," what a gathering of the faithful that will be!

When the golden harps are sounding, and the angel bands proclaim, in triumphant strains the glorious jubilee; then to meet and join to sing the song of Moses and the Lamb, what a gathering of the faithful that will be!

J.H. Kurzenknabe

Acts 1:8

"But you shall receive power when the Holy Spirit has come upon you; and you shall be witnesses to Me in Jerusalem, and in Judea and Samaria, and to the end of the earth."

Joel 2:1-2

Blow the trumpet in Zion, and sound an alarm in My holy mountain! Let all the inhabitants of the land tremble; for the day of the Lord is coming, for it is at hand: A day of darkness and gloominess, a day of clouds and thick darkness, like the morning clouds spread over the mountains. A people come, great and strong, the like of whom has never been; nor will there ever be any such after them, even for many successive generations.

Joel 2:12-13

Now, therefore, says the Lord, Turn to Me with all your heart, with fasting, with weeping, and with mourning. So rend your heart and not your garments; return to the Lord your God, for He is gracious and merciful, slow to anger, and of great kindness; and he relents from doing harm.

Joel 2:28

And it shall come to pass afterward that I will pour out My Spirit on all flesh; your sons and your daughters shall prophesy, your old men shall dream dreams, your young men shall see visions; and also on My menservants and My maidservants I will pour out My Spirit in those days. And I will show wonders in the heavens and in the earth: blood and fire and pillars of smoke. The sun shall be turned into darkness, and the moon into blood, before the coming of the great and terrible day of the Lord. And it shall come to pass that whosoever calls on the name of the Lord shall be saved. For in Mount Zion and in Jerusalem there shall be deliverance, as the Lord has said, among the remnant whom the Lord calls."

Ezekiel 3:16-19

Now it came to pass at the end of seven days that the word of the Lord came to me, saying, Son of man, I have made you a watchman for the house of Israel; therefore hear a word from My mouth, and give them warning from Me: When I say to the wicked, You shall surely die, and you give him no warning, nor speak to warn the wicked from this wicked way, to save his life, that same wicked man shall die in his iniquity; but his blood I will require at your hand. Yet, if you warn the wicked and he does not turn from his wickedness, nor from his wicked way, he shall die in his iniquity; but you have delivered your soul.

Romans 3:23

For all have sinned and fall short of the Glory of God,

Romans 6:23

For the wages of sin is death, but the gift of God is eternal life in Christ Jesus our Lord.

Romans 5:8

But God demonstrates His own love toward us, in that while we were still sinners, Christ died for us.

Romans 10:9-10

That if you confess with your mouth the Lord Jesus and believe in your heart that God has raised Him from the dead, you will be saved. For with the heart one believes to righteousness, and with the mouth confession is made to salvation.

Romans 10:13

For whoever calls upon the name of the Lord shall be saved.

Matthew 28:19-20

"Go therefore and make disciples of all nations, baptizing them in the name of the Father and of the Son and of the Holy Spirit, teaching them to observe all things that I have commanded; and lo, I am with you always, and even to the end of the age."

John 14:6

Jesus said to him, I am the way, the truth, and the life. No one comes to the Father except through Me.

John 15:13

Greater love has no one than this, than to lay down one's life for his friends.

Revelation 22:12

And behold, I'm coming quickly, and My reward is with Me, to give to every one according to his work.

Isaiah 40:3-5

The voice of one crying in the wilderness: Prepare the way of the Lord; make straight in the desert a highway for our God. Every valley shall be exalted and every mountain and hill brought low; the crooked places shall be made straight and the rough places smooth; the glory of the Lord shall be revealed, and all flesh shall see it together; for the mouth of the Lord has spoken.

<u>A Special Thanks</u>

I want to give a special thanks to the Mission America Team, Jill Campbell, Rhonda Butcher, Kaweah Stines and Beverly Maes, who labored and worked faithfully everyday. Great is your reward.

And as we continue to labor in the harvest field with A Touch From Above - Prayer Mountain and Mission San Diego, California. Your labor is not in vain. God bless you.

Dr. Luauna Stines

Connect with Dr. Luauna Stines

Facebook: Dr. Luauna Stines

Facebook: A Touch From Above Prayer Mountain

Twitter: @DrLuaunaStines

YouTube: Dr. Luauna Stines

Write Dr. Luauna Stines-P.O Box 2800 –Ramona, CA 92065

Email: PastorLuauna@ATouchFromAbove.org

Email: DrLuauna@ATouchFromAbove.org

ATouchFromAbove.org

About the Author

Dr. Luauna Stines is Founder and President of A Touch From Above, LSM Inc. Her goal is to reach the world, and hurting people with her story of God's amazing grace; a testimony of hope and victory, a murdered husband, betrayal of marriage, and a devastating drug addiction. A drastic change happened in Dr. Luauna Stines' life when she had a collision with Truth, the Gospel Of Jesus Christ.

She is the author of A Mother's Story – Part One, A Mother's Story Part Two, Mission America and Golden Nuggets.

Now ministering over 34 years, Dr. Stines received an honorary doctorate from the I.M.I. Bible College & Seminary; a District Ministerial License from LIFE Bible College of the International Church of the Foursquare Gospel. She also holds an education certificate in Ministry Training and Development from Oral Roberts University.

Dr. Stines is an Evangelist, Teacher, and Preacher, she has preached the gospel throughout the world, in South Korea, (former) Yugoslavia, Italy, Australia, England, Germany, Switzerland, Mexico, Central Africa, and the United States. In her travels, she has also preached for the satellite churches of Dr. Yonggi Cho of the Yoido Full Gospel Church in Seoul, Pusan, Chonju and Inchon, located in South Korea.

Preaching on television in San Diego, California, Dr. Luauna Stines touches the hearts of thousands with a simple pure message, "When You are Hardest Hit, Don't Quit" A Touch From Above - Dr. Luauna Stines, also ministers on radio every Sunday morning at 9 a.m. on KPRZ 1210 AM in San Diego, California.

She is the founder of Victorious Homes for Men and Women, a discipleship program which has had over 500 men and women come through the program for over 20 years in Colorado, Oregon, and now preparing to open homes in Southern California.

Dr. Stines is building Prayer Mountain, a Christian Prayer Center & Bible School in Ramona, CA, in the heart of San Diego County. She has dedicated 25 acres of land for God's people to train, learn to pray and trust God to answer all their needs.

Returning from Seoul, Korea with a burden in her heart, "We need a place for God's people to pray in the USA." She knew it would take great faith for the walls of prayer to be rebuilt in America. Not just a whisper, but the effective, fervent prayer of a righteous man or woman that availeth much. The Prayer Mountain is now being built, and ministers and saints alike are coming to seek the Lord in prayer.

She is a weekly columnist appearing in the East County Gazette and has a blog on _drluauna.com_. Her website is _ATouchFromAbove.org_

Dr. Luauna Stines is the mother of two children now grown, and a proud grandmother of four.

www.ingramcontent.com/pod-product-compliance
Lightning Source LLC
Chambersburg PA
CBHW070345090426
42733CB00009B/1296